# HEART-LINKS

*Inspiring Personal*
*Stories That Explore*
*Our Powerful Ability*
*to Communicate with*
*Our Lost Loved Ones*

LOUISE PLATT HAUCK

Council Oak Books
San Francisco / Tulsa

*To Mindy*
*among the awakened children*

For information regarding Louise Hauck's travel schedule,
seminars, workshops and consultations, please contact

Illuminations
511 6th Avenue, Ste. 234
New York, NY 10011
(212) 645-2335
SeeBYond@aol.com
www.visitilluminations.com

Council Oak Books, LLC
1290 Chestnut Street, Ste 2, San Francisco, CA 94109
1350 E. 15th Street, Tulsa, OK 74120
HEART-LINKS: *Inspiring Personal Stories That Explore Our Powerful Ability to Communicate with Our Lost Loved Ones.* Copyright © 2000 by Louise Platt Hauck. All rights reserved.

**Library of Congress Cataloging-in-Publication Data**

Hauck, Louise Platt, 1946–
    Heart-links : inspiring personal stories that explore our powerful ability to communicate with our lost loved ones / Louise Platt Hauck.—1st ed.
        p.cm.
    ISBN 1-57178-092-0
    1. Spiritualism—Case studies. I. Title.
    BF1261.2.H38 2000
    133.9'3—dc21                                         99-087109

First edition / First printing.
Printed in Canada.
00 01 02 03 04 05 06   5 4 3 2 1

# Contents

# Preface

*I* was eleven years old when I saw my first vision. It might have been a Friday night, since I was sleeping on the pull-out sofa in the upstairs family room. Had it been a school night, I would have been in my own bed, in my own room.

I made a special effort to brush my teeth carefully before bed, because I'd popped myself some popcorn earlier in the evening. My father engineered a neat, efficient "popcorn stand" on a TV tray in the corner of the family room: popper, glass jar of kernels, paper towels and special coconut oil—his answer to the secret for "theater-tasting" popcorn. I must have eaten two or three bowls full.

My father built the family room himself. When you reached the landing at the top of the stairs you had to push open the double doors, then step down two or three steps. The large windows around the family room always rattled if you stepped down too hard. That night I walked slowly and softly. The movie

I'd watched ended very late, and I didn't want to awaken the rest of my family.

I was returning from the bathroom, walking carefully past the large window on my right. Suddenly I felt pulled over to it, compelled to look out into a beautiful, glowing, moonlit night. The moon was full, looking extra bright and washed after a heavy rain. The puffy clouds were illuminated by its glow. The whole sky looked magical.

I cranked open both sides of the window, letting in the fragrant cool, damp night air. I felt overwhelmed by the rush of sensations that complemented the visual images of the sky and moon. Then I did what I've come to do in years since, whenever I feel moved and overwhelmed by nature's beauty, or by the perfection of how things fit together in life: I began reciting the Lord's Prayer, softly, to myself. At the time, it was the most reverent and holy response I could think of making.

"Our Father, which art in heaven, hallowed be thy name," I began. Suddenly the clouds began to move, first slowly, then briskly, sweeping away to the right. Then they returned to the same space in the sky, now forming what looked like an outdoor stage setting, the kind that would enhance a presentation of Shakespeare or light opera on a summer evening. I blinked twice, trying to clear the vision emerging before me.

The clouds formed a throne, surrounded by distinct images of trees, hills and valleys. The light of the moon now beamed directly onto the throne; a celestial confirmation spoke to me, saying, "Yes, God the Father is here."

A chill ran through me and I continued, more moved than shaken: "Thy kingdom come, thy will be done, on earth as it is in heaven." Again, the clouds swept over to the right in the sky, then returned to form another vignette.

I watched a new scene form: shepherds standing in a pasture, leaning on staffs and looking up to the light, even brighter now, which illuminated the detailed features of their faces. In that moment, I knew that I was on earth to help bring heaven to earth. I gave thanks for being guided on such a mission.

Seemingly in response to my thanks, the clouds once more moved away and returned again, this time forming a circle around the moon, conveying to me the perfect arrangement of the higher order of our life plans. What I then understood intuitively was that while on one level life appears mysterious and bewildering, on another, glimpses of the greater picture and understanding of our purpose are attainable.

At that point, I ran—no longer caring whom I disturbed— to get my mother. We were accustomed to sharing spiritual (not necessarily religious) ideas, and now I wanted to share my vision. I woke her, and she followed me back into the family room and over to the window.

The vision was gone. We looked out at a normal nighttime sky—pretty moon, puffy clouds. Then my mother bestowed one of the greatest gifts she could have given me.

"Sweetheart," she said, "it must have been just for you."

In that moment, she reflected back to me her trust in my ability to see beyond the obvious in this physical world. I am blessed that my mother reflected my own light back to me, showing me where to find it within myself. That has allowed me to nurture the light and share its gifts with the world.

# Acknowledgments

My thanks to contributing clients who reached into deep and vulnerable places to recount their stories. The inevitability of *Heart-Links'* publication was demonstrated by its synchronistic ride from Sandra Martin to the talented people at Council Oak Books.

This book moved speedily and synchronistically on its way with eleventh-hour efforts from Pat Barrentine, CJ Conner and John Hughes. Jaene Leonard, Glenn Levy, Cindy Mayfield, Polly Lazaron and Jan Pikowsky reassured me that this book, and my presence on the planet, are necessary. Beloved coordinators around the world have cheered me on with love in generous, openhearted ways.

Joe Spigelman and Harry Fishkin made New York City a safe and friendly place. My children Adrianne/Rochel Ruth and Dylan continue to teach me the value of loving and releasing them to their own destinies. My family loves me, even when they don't see what I see; my niece, Greta—who does see—supports me with deliberate intention.

Thank you one and all. I am humbled by your faith in me and your never-ceasing love and generosity.

# Introduction

When I was four years old, I said to my mother, "When you go to heaven, we'll write letters!" I couldn't know then that I was receiving an intuitive insight from the future alerting me to a very important aspect of my life's eventual work. I would be able to stay in touch, to interpret for souls who had completed their allotted time in this dimension, to help maintain the connection for those who were left behind. My mother and I did stay in touch after her death. When my daughter was very young, she experienced meetings with my mother while she slept. They chatted about events and memories that only Mother and I had shared. The details that my daughter related about these meetings gave me great comfort. To know that my dear mother could still communicate and that she had gotten to know her granddaughter—though she had never met her in the physical world—showed me that our heart connections linked all three of us beyond death.

My ability to communicate with my parents, both of whom died relatively young—at age fifty-one—didn't bring them back to me. I can still find that pain, that hollow feeling of loss. But my intuitive abilities have expanded my perceptions about life, death, and a Higher Power and a larger, more purposeful, plan. We receive gifts from each of the challenges life presents. If we can allow these challenges to expand our perceptions, to help us grow spiritually, the Universe will connect us to those who need our insight. The Universe eventually sends us those with whom we are to share these gifts.

At one point in my attempt to understand how it is that I am able to see clairvoyantly beyond the illusions of death and linear time, I approached physicists with questions. I was gathering some interesting information, when two individuals came forward to caution me, "You do not need physics or science to define your work! Let it stand alone!" These two people were the late Willis Harman, past president of the Institute of Noetic Sciences and author of several new paradigm books, and Gary Zukav, author of *The Dancing Wu Li Masters* and *The Seat of the Soul.*

Their message influenced the route my work and my writing have taken. I am continually shaping both my work and my writing to respond effectively to a growing hunger folks have today for information that may not be scientifically proven nor quantifiably defined, but which revives their spiritual identity and offers an expanded view of life that is down to earth, practical, relevant and immediately useful.

These people are wrestling with frustrations and disillusionment over all that their lives don't contain. I've helped many of them to awaken from illusion and integrate a new understanding of reality. My efforts are aimed at responding to this new eagerness and receptivity to becoming fully integrated, multisensory (trusting beyond the five senses), spiritual beings.

The single most important message of my work, and this book, is this: We've been misinformed about death. It doesn't exist, except as it concerns our bodies and other matter that wears away over time. The soul, energized by our spirit—our life force—is indeed eternal. It makes an endless journey through lifetimes, showing up for adventures that expand us in love and sometimes contract us in fear. Some of our experiences have enabled us to soar to greater heights, and others have tempted us with choices that spiraled us downward into darkness.

We come into this dimension to experience both the light and the dark. When we embrace both of these powerful forces within ourselves, acknowledging that our souls are vulnerable to the darkness of fear, greed, selfishness, jealousy, abuse, addictions, self-absorption—to name a few of the effects of our less-wise choices—we can awaken to these very important realizations:

- As life continually challenges us, sometimes in unimaginable ways, we can choose to use the same free will that can get us in to so much karma-creating trouble to make more conscious, illuminated choices in every moment. Wiser choices direct us toward more expansive, positive experiences.
- We are the sum total of all our experiences. The effects of both kinds of choices go with us beyond the death of the body into eternity, as the soul seeks balance and resolution. So, too, go the love, the memories and the humor.
- "Grace" can turn our lives around on a dime. Grace is an instantaneous bestowal of forgiveness and unconditional love that expands us to the farthest reaches of our timeless

existence. It's a gift that we receive from the infinite Source when we take personal responsibility for our actions, actively seek balance and resolution, and then surrender—release our expectations of anticipated outcomes and give up our futile attempts at scriptwriting our life's plan—to the Source.

- Our soul is the generator that runs old programs, "soul memories," and our spirit is the spark that carries forth the good, the bad, the ugly and the beauty of all that we've embraced and chosen in each life.

My work as a clairvoyant "seer" has been my heartfelt pleasure and my greatest teacher. I am blessed to do this "work." It is my joy to collect perspectives that shed light on the seemingly unanswerable, provide solace for the inconsolable, give me greater courage to share my insights and strengthen my faith in the face of the unpredictable.

Much like an antenna picks up signals, I receive messages from "departed" souls, the ever-eternal loved ones and relatives of my clients. These souls are vibrantly "alive." The lack of physical form in no way diminishes their connection with those they love. Their messages are filled with humor, deep affection, detailed memories, puns, personal jokes and invaluable confirmation of our timeless nature.

For over fifteen years, I have observed—personally and professionally—hundreds of people around the world whose lives really do make sense within a greater plan. In many cases, when I see new faces in my audiences at bookstores and various speaking venues, or as first-time clients, I learn they have just experienced the death of a loved one. What seems to be overwhelming grief becomes an opportunity to change in unforeseen ways. They discover that the heart connection to those they have lost—sometimes stretching through many lifetimes—that makes the physical missing so unbearable, is the very same connection that continues to link them to those souls on the Other Side.

Many of these people are beginning to learn that they, too, can be receivers of highly intuitive information, of subtle or startling messages from the Other Side. We are all members of a still evolving multidimensional, multisensing species. My clients and students demonstrate this in their stories that follow.

I want to express my gratitude to my clients—to their eternal, never-ending souls—for their stories and their wonderful (and often inspiring) willingness to grow and expand from their personal challenges, challenges that often include the heartbreaking loss of a loved one. It is my privilege to greet them on their paths, as they follow their souls' natural inclination to seek resolution and balance, even in one lifetime. It is to those seekers that I dedicate *Heart-Links*.

A few words about terminology, since the words that I (and my clients) have chosen will have certain meanings to the reader, particularly when they connect to important, personal beliefs. I am respectful of the fact that my clients—and my readers—hold many differing religious and spiritual beliefs, and refer to a Supreme Being in their own, respective ways.

For example, I find that my religious Jewish clients refer to the concept of a Supreme Being as "Hashem" (meaning, "the name") rather than to diminish the greatness that it represents by even uttering the name of "G-d." My Native American clients call God "the Breathmaker," and clients who feel that using "God" gives spiritual pursuits a religious flavoring prefer "the Source." I usually use "the Source" when I refer to God, or a Higher Power.

I refer to "the Other Side" but hesitate to do so, because it implies a place "over there" or some "where" that we go between our earthly experiences. Although it's a bit lengthy, I usually prefer to use "the nonphysical dimension," in an attempt to stretch the reader into a perception of our eternal souls as not being limited to time, place or space.

I mention souls who have "made their transition," "left their physical bodies," have "passed over," or "died." I use these terms interchangeably.

Maybe one day, when there is more of a consensus about the existence of an energy that is infinitely greater than our "selves" and about the illusion of death—where we do (or don't) "go" and how we get "there"—the words we use will be simpler.

# CHAPTER ONE

# Losing a Loved One

*T*he loss of a loved one is always devastating. From the moment a medical prognosis alerts family members to the possibility of death, anticipation of that loss can throw lives into a tailspin well in advance of the loved one's departure.

Along with the grief can come anger, when we realize that our expectations about life were misleading. We wonder how it can be that our loved ones won't be traveling with us for our entire "tour of duty" in this physical dimension. Fear is often triggered as we are forced to acknowledge that this is not a permanent excursion for ourselves either. For some, day-to-day life can become filled with lamentations over what would have been, what could have been and what will never be. The future becomes a fearful prospect.

I observe my clients' reactions toward death as I travel throughout the United States and Europe, Australia, New Zealand, and Israel. On cruises and by phone, I've worked with individuals from Canada, Scotland, Switzerland, Italy, Austria, Germany, Greece, Greenland, Singapore, South Africa, Iraq, Iran and South America. I'm finding on a global scale that my clients are experiencing a more open attitude about death. I'm watching a growing number of souls experience death—their own as well as others'—as more of a transitional phase, a passage to a freer, more expansive existence, and as part of a continuum where contact with loved ones, colleagues and teachers can still be maintained.

As many of these clients gain this new perspective, they are learning a whole new set of responses to the anticipation and the experience of death. Acceptance of death as a natural phase of the soul's journey is starting to replace old beliefs that death is a bad thing happening, a fearful occurrence. With less fear surrounding the prospect of the inevitable death of the body, I find that people are more able to pay attention to life in the present. They are learning to live more fully in each precious moment.

As they become more present, these individuals also become appreciative of all that goes on around them and are less distracted by issues from the past and fears of the future. They recognize more acutely the gifts that result from their challenges. And they notice many more road signs, or "synchronicities" (seemingly psychic timing of events), guiding them down their paths. My clients are making wiser, more conscious choices for themselves and are taking more responsibility for those choices by becoming attentive observers of their own lives.

Awakened individuals feel less fear, and my clients talk to me about having faith in and gratitude for an infinite and perfect plan, even when life seems unresponsive to their own personal will. Expressions of gratitude are replacing cries of frustration. Faith in a greater plan allows us to surrender to the Source well before life's circumstances force a more abrupt letting go.

For those who have experienced this kind of awakening and letting go, the unexpected or imminent death of a loved one can be met with greater equanimity and an increased ability to bring comfort to others. Challenging circumstances call their gifts into action. They are feeling more prepared to sit with and comfort the dying. They are able to participate in the process as a celebration, rather than running away and hiding in denial and fear.

They tell me about the gifts that they have received when they've allowed themselves to be close to one who is dying. In some cases, they have been able to see what a loved one saw in his or her last hours, breathing into the rhythm of that life-changing experience. They treasure the thoughts and reflections shared in the final moments, whether the loved one is conscious or not! And most importantly, they become a participant in the joy and freedom that occurs when the restrictions of the physical body no longer inhibit their loved one and he or she is released.

Experiencing the predicted, unexpected or imminent death of a loved one can deepen our experience of life. The stories in this book give evidence of the shift in consciousness I've observed. These are personal accounts from clients who are trusting the "nudges" that urge them to perceive life from an expanded perspective. Their experiences—along with some of my own—will show how they are learning to trust their ability to see and sense more, and expand their perceptions beyond the illusion of time and death. They are elated to find that they have never lost their connection with departed loved ones. When they remember the love shared—and feel that feeling—their hearts open and they instantly access the magical link between two worlds.

## Spirit Transitions

We are eternal beings. We are energy. Energy does not end. It transforms, but it doesn't end. As I have said, the most important element of my work lies in debunking old beliefs about death and releasing people from their fear of it. In the consultations, I also serve as interpreter for souls who come forward from the Other Side to communicate to loved ones through me. These are souls who have passed from their physical bodies and have gone to the Light.

I've been asked to de-haunt a few dwellings, but I don't do "ghost-busting" for lost souls—those caught between dimensions who haven't made it to the Light. Just as I tend to attract awakening souls as clients on this side, only those on the Other Side who have been through "orientation" and are engaged in meaningful reflections and learning are the ones who are invited and "escorted" to join us in the consultations.

When the earthly experience of a soul ends violently, that soul often arrives on the Other Side in a state of confusion or bewilderment. Souls often need a period of rest. When suicide victims realize they have short-stopped a valuable opportunity for growth by ending their lives, they tend to rush back in, only to repeat the same mistakes. Prayers on their behalf do support them in gaining new tools that will prompt wiser choices upon their return.

Some souls, who live and die in a more awakened state, tend to arrive on the Other Side more conscious and alert.

Guides and angels escort some souls to consultations to heal and resolve issues. Other souls know the way.

Our evolving soul never stops learning. When we make our transition into spirit, we meet with teachers, attend classes, contribute to special projects, share in groups and learn from reflecting back on our lives. I joke that there is even "AA" (Alcoholics Anonymous) on the Other Side.

Souls come through telepathically to assist with the healing of loved ones, to help validate the client by taking responsibility for a part they have played in the past—thereby balancing karmic issues for them both—and to confirm that they haven't "died." They also demonstrate that love is never lost, and sometimes they convey feelings that they were unable to communicate in the physical plane.

Souls often project memories a client will recognize. One client met with an old Air Force buddy in a consultation. His friend had passed over a few years before. He pantomimed a flight maneuver that my client would recognize. Then his friend reminded him of the beautiful sunrises that they used to view from the air.

## Etheric Intervention Healing

A psychologist once asked me to make a presentation and then "tune in" to a group of her clients who met on a weekly basis. I took time to describe themes that each group member was working on and growing from—from my perspective—and interpreted for some souls (usually family) from the Other Side who came to help with the process of resolving old issues.

When I was done, the therapist confirmed that I had covered most of the issues that each client was working with in private sessions. Then she said, "What you're doing is called intervention!" I might refer to this aspect of my work as "etheric mediation" or "etheric intervention." It often involves facilitating a healing between the perpetrator of past sexual or physical abuse and the victim, my client.

A client in Virginia had suffered four concussions at the hands of his father, now deceased, before the age of seven. When I receive sensory data telepathically, I have to interpret the information in the clearest, most meaningful way. The skill, for me, is not in viewing and sensing the information, but in relating it meaningfully and concisely.

I saw a large hand, taking a swipe. (When there has been sexual abuse, I'm usually shown a groping hand.) I merged with the father's consciousness, accessible beyond time, and experienced many of his feelings in the early years of raising his son. I felt his self-loathing, his impatience with his sensitive, nonathletic son and his awkwardness in showing love or affection. I could see that his father had beaten him in his childhood.

I felt his regrets about the past as well as his heart, now open and yearning to reach out to his son. Then I heard his words in thoughts. I interpreted all of this in the following way:

"Your father is saying, 'Please know that the way I treated you was not a true reflection of your worth. I loathed myself for my inability to meet *my* father's expectations. I projected that self-scorn onto you. If I could make you perfect, then I would absolve myself. You were a very sensitive child and you asked a lot of questions that I didn't know how to answer. You spoke from your feelings. When you conveyed feelings, that made me feel confused. My father beat his expectations into me and I shut down from feeling before you were born. Feelings terrified me. Now it feels easier to open my heart. Please receive my love. You are loved. I used to call you 'sissy.' You are the courageous one. Let's stop this cycle of self-loathing and abuse. Your healing is my healing.'"

It felt as though my client's father had been escorted to the reading for a special project, a field trip, to work through unfinished business with his son. These kinds of sessions serve as confirmation that we are all in this together, whether in or out of the body.

## Collaboration between Two Realities

Increasingly I'm observing a shift in the focus of the messages that indicate how we'll be working together in these two realities. For years the most important messages for clients from deceased loved ones were assurances such as these: "I'm with your mother now, and I was with you in the garden last week when you were trimming the rosebushes." "Your sister may have gotten my pearls, but you got the greatest gift—knowing the love between us is never lost." "Don't fight about the burial details—I'm no longer in that body." "I defined myself by my possessions, but now I'm free and can see much farther."

Now it seems that just as we—on this side—are being encouraged to trust our own intuition about our increasing roles as multisensory beings, there are new projects and opportunities for souls on the Other Side. Some souls take on the role of guides, encouraging clients to trust their ability to receive telepathic communication as they learn to transmit from the Other Side. We're going to be working together in times ahead. The veil that separates the physical and nonphysical dimensions is coming down.

When I do readings with nurses, the room often fills up with souls who want to convey how intuitive the caregiver's thoughts and deeds were when my clients tended to them before their passing. Bob was a patient who had suffered with AIDS. He came forward from the Other Side to thank his past nurse—my client Karla—for her special loving touch when he was near death. He sent me the telepathic image of a long stalk of something in a vase on his hospital bedside table. Karla remembered Bob; having discovered in his records that he was a farmer, she had once lovingly placed a stalk of wheat in his room.

Bob also thanked her for knowing just the right moment at which to escort his family from his hospital room so he could concentrate and "face forward" for the journey ahead. He wanted her to know that her thoughts had helped direct him to the Light. He encouraged her to trust her ability to do that for patients.

This example is one of many such messages I'm receiving and interpreting from souls on the Other Side. The grieving process is an important and necessary one for loved ones who are "left behind." Mourning the painful physical absence of one you have known and loved is very much a part of your earthly experience. Through the healing process you gain the understanding that life is ever changing and that life goes on. Eventually it allows us to release those who have made their transition to the Other Side.

Experiencing our own personal grief doesn't necessarily hold souls back. Feelings of unresolved anger, blame and abandonment are often part of the healing process. While we move through our own stages of grieving and healing, souls who pass over also move through their own process of orientation, review and reflection. They are still the same evolving souls. They may be able to view life from a broader perspective, but they don't suddenly rise to some sort of guruhood or necessarily know what's best for you any more than you know for yourself.

This common urge to bring Light into the world through healing and resolution, rather than merely intruding into the physical or nonphysical dimensions, is the ongoing project through which we and our spirit loved ones will grow together.

## Rescuing Another

Clients are often in tremendous pain when they first come to me for a consultation. Instinctively—or reflexively—I'm tempted to rush in and announce the good news: "Guess what! You're loved one didn't die! I'll give you evidence!"

To do so would be a reaction to my own fear of feeling so much pain. My more enlightened self has learned that we have no right to take away another's pain. We grow from our pain when we resist the temptation to feel victimized.

It is extremely important for one who has suffered the loss of a loved one to move through every stage of the grief process and not be distracted into denial by "good news." Any attempt to rescue another disempowers that person and leaves him with a lack of faith in his own ability to find answers and heal over time.

I've learned how very important it is to acknowledge my clients' pain, rather than attempt to save them from it. Life challenges us to expand from our pain. It certainly does get our attention. Therefore, when I meet with a client who is grieving, I search my heart to retrieve the feelings of loss that I have felt in my own life, and then proceed with (and pray for) sensitivity and compassion.

That said, I do love—and am blessed—to be a deliverer of hope, presenting evidence that what we perceive as an ending is simply a transitional phase in the continuum of eternal life.

## NOTHING TO SAVE ME FROM

*This client's account shows how one couple responded to a terminal diagnosis by continuing to experience the best that life could offer. It also shows how their relationship deepened.*

My husband, Gene, had been diagnosed as having multiple myeloma—a persistent, though not aggressive, form of bone marrow cancer—five years before his death on January 22, 1993. We accepted this news as useful information, not a death sentence, even though the doctor told him, "We can't say, 'Good, we caught it early,' because we don't know what to do to cure you." Immediately Gene began a healing journey of nutritional support, complementary health care with doctors practicing nontraditional medicine and his own meditations and inner healing. And he stayed on the job in his second career as a remodeling contractor, which he loved.

An amazing man, Gene intended to live life to the fullest regardless of doctors' predictions. He told people, "I was depressed for a couple days, but that weakens my immune system and I need all the help I can get." For the most part Gene felt good, maintained an active life finishing construction of our new home, playing golf, walking, enjoying reading and some travel. Always an active person, he learned to pace himself as time went by, and rested more frequently. If or when he was in any pain, he did his best not to show it.

Gene and I met in the sixth grade, so we had been best friends for a long time. We simply did not allow the reality of our life together coming to a conclusion to dominate our remaining time with each other, though Gene did express his sense of pending loss on a couple of special occasions.

On our fortieth anniversary, he wrote:

"40 years—
Such a short time
to be best friends
to love completely
to create success
to honor each other
to build
to have family
to enjoy life
to heal
to be
Such a short time
40 years."

For our forty-first anniversary, he wrote: "Thank you for these forty-one wonderful years. For the love, the caring and most important of all, the friendship. If, by the grace of God we are given another year together I shall find joy in each moment." And we did celebrate our forty-second anniversary on September 2, 1992.

Toward the end of that year, his activity was made more difficult following a fall while gardening that fractured three vertebrae. With the help of chiropractic and other healing plus a wraparound brace, he could still play some golf for most of the year.

Accepting this new challenge, he was determined to add joy to his life by doing what he loved—playing trumpet again after thirty years. He bought a new horn and practiced for six months to get his lip back, then joined the county concert band. He also made wooden toys for our grandchildren and for donation to the Christmas bureau.

In November 1992, his blood work showed some changes. A chemist by training, he knew what he was looking at and I sensed a change in his confidence, though he didn't tell me what he suspected. Looking back, I can see that Gene knew he was approaching the end of his time here.

We heard about a doctor who had moved his practice to Mexico, as have many effective practitioners who go against the AMA protocols. This man had been successful in treating very difficult back problems as well as enhancing the immune system. Treatments were for seven weeks, three days each time.

We couldn't fly, as Gene had developed an ear infection over the holidays. So, the day after New Year's, we drove from our home northeast of Sacramento to San Ysidro on the Mexican border, and took a van across to Tijuana to see this doctor. Three days later we drove home—a thirteen-hour trip. The driving was difficult and yet Gene was determined to give this a try. Then, home for three days and back on the road.

At the time, I was editing a quarterly business journal and, when home, I did my best to stay current with my work.

Returning from our third trip on Tuesday night, Gene was particularly tired. Next morning it was clear that he wasn't doing well and I suggested taking him to the hospital. "They'd only kill me" was his reply. So he rested in his lounge chair and I hurried to get the blueline copy corrected to send back to the journal printer, knowing that if Gene were in the hospital my work would not get done at all.

Wednesday night he didn't have the muscle strength to get up the stairs to bed, and so he slept in his chair and I slept nearby on the couch. By Thursday noon, I determined we had to go to the hospital. Gene was having trouble breathing and so was not getting enough oxygen, and we had a ninety-minute drive to the hospital. Angels drove with us for sure. He stopped breathing about thirty minutes after they got him in the emergency room and I approved using a ventilator, telling them not to do anything heroic if his heart was failing. I called Louise, whom we had known for a couple years, as well as our three children. My oldest son in San Diego said, "I'll be there in three hours."

Next morning I made a quick trip home while our son stayed with Gene. Other times when he had been in the hospital and our children asked, "Is he going to be okay?", I'd check and tell them, "Yes, I can see him back home." When I walked in the door this time, the house felt empty and I knew he wasn't coming home. To confirm my intuition, there was a message from Louise saying, "I see a reception line forming." In a reading the previous year she had told me, "He'll have the time he needs."

Gene died twenty-four hours after arriving at the hospital. Our son and I each told him good-bye, that it was okay to leave and how much we loved him. Being there as he drew his last breath was a deeply spiritual experience for me.

Louise called later that night to say Gene had popped in saying, "I didn't know how ready I was. How wonderful it is to be free from pain." This was a special blessing.

When Louise visited a couple months later and we did a session, of course Gene was right there, saying, "Now the journey begins—yours and mine." And, while I didn't feel any guilt for not having taken him to the hospital earlier, I was puzzled as to why the seriousness of his condition just was not apparent to me. It almost felt like I was blocked in some way. So I asked. His reply was so helpful. "If you had seen the larger picture, you might have rescued me—as if there was anything to save me from." He also told me that while I was stroking his forehead, saying good-bye, he was standing behind me holding me.

I have never doubted that there is life after death and knew Gene would find things to do that he loved in what many of us refer to as "heaven." After reading *Testimony of Light* by Helen Greaves, he was pleased with the idea that there was something to do on the "Other Side." Through Louise I asked him if his experience was similar to Greaves's reports and he said, "Yes, though a bit different." Over time, through Louise, I learned that Gene was involved in his spirit life in scientific and engineering activities. His group was working on "devices" to facilitate communications between the two dimensions. "Sort of like fiber optics," he said.

In a later session, Louise explained, "It's almost like he has a tunnel going from him to you—like a corridor. And as he has said before, he's in class learning about transmitting energy on his end. It's as if you have two people on opposite ends building a railroad track and one's in Nebraska and one's in California and they are building toward each other and at some point the railroad track will connect."

*Pat Barrentine*

## Recreating, Retracing, Repositioning

Many of what we think are new events in our lives are actually replays that represent where we've been in past earthly adventures. Our childhood, life circumstances and challenges effectively set the stage to reposition us, to awaken us and to allow us to make new choices. We recreate past scenarios to stimulate the soul memory of past themes—feats accomplished and opportunities missed—and to remind us to move on from where we left off.

However, sometimes people misinterpret a soul memory as a cue to act again in an old way. I've counseled more than one client who thought they had found their soul mate, even though the one they'd met was married to another, raising several children. They took the strong feelings of familiarity with that person as a sure sign that they were meant to be together. In such cases, I usually find that they are remembering a relationship that has already been. Then I'm shown a past life that confirms this.

"Why do you think you both set it up this way, to be so unavailable to each other this time?" I asked Beth, a client I was seeing for the first time. A consultant for a large computer corporation, she was frustrated by her attraction to Bill, a married man with four children.

During her reading, I described a past-life overlay. In the other life space, they lived a long life together in France. She supported him in his political endeavors, making socially correct maneuvers that promoted his success. She was also dedicated to raising their three boys and two girls.

Beth's deathbed scene showed her beloved husband and most of the children at her bedside. She died in peace, fulfilled, but curious about other potentials she might have explored.

"Your life was most likely staged this way to prompt you both to allow your relationship to transform and create something new," I told her. "Perhaps your past connection will lead you to a friendship that stimulates creativity—implementation of an innovative idea—or supports greater spiritual depth in each other."

Existing conditions in the supposed partners' lives are simply road signs for them to interpret. Indeed, karmic drama can tempt players to play again, to repeat old patterns and choices. I believe, however, that we are evolving too quickly and expanding too greatly in this lifetime to give in to karmic pulls. When we go to the Light and reflect back on our life, we may regret that we missed new opportunities by repeating old choices.

## Past Selves Send Their Gifts

Beyond the illusion of time, you still exist in this life's past and coexist in other life spaces. The past exists simultaneously with the present. Sometimes it's helpful to look at past lives metaphorically. Past selves can represent aspects of you that are ready to die in peace, excess baggage you don't have to carry into your future. Hypnotherapy, past-life regressions and guided meditations can assist in confirming what fears and unfinished business you're returned to heal and resolve.

Past selves also have gifts to send you. They hold aspects of your timeless essence to be reawakened—talents, creative potentials and courage that are still accessible. For example, a while ago I discovered that I am my own grandmother. My father named me after her—his mother. She died in 1943 and I was born in 1946. Some feel that when a soul returns that quickly, it is either very drawn to this physical dimension, or it comes for a specific mission. In my case, the first possibility is probably less true than the second.

My grandmother/myself was the writer of eighty books and three hundred short stories. She was also the historian for the Pony Express in St. Joseph, Missouri. Her passion for writing was such that she frequently read all day and wrote into the night. She supported three families through the Great Depression with her writing. The pressure caused too many sleepless nights, prompting her to take sleeping pills for much needed rest. The habit eventually necessitated a short stay in a sanitarium.

My first job—this lifetime—was in a mental hospital, where I worked as a music therapist and researcher. It seems that events in this life might have positioned me to say, "Let's see here, where did I leave off?"

It's amusing to me to think that I got along so much better with my mother as her daughter than I did as her mother-in-law. A faint soul memory also sometimes reminds me—beyond time—of the admiration that I felt for my daughter-in-law's (my mother's) spiritual radiance. I remember it as being a little intimidating and wanting to explore that—inevitably—as her daughter.

Trusting that I carry some lingering writing potential from that past Louise, soul memories have helped me interpret that my focus this incarnation is to include more of a spiritual emphasis, previously lacking. Soul memories also help explain intermittent fears I have about writing—that the intensity of the creative process could swallow me up. It's important not to attach too closely to any past self or life we've been or lived. We are expanding now, to be greater than any self we've ever been. But it's helpful to be aware of our timeless aspects—still accessible—to trust the potentials and overcome the fears.

I lived for three years at the foot of the Colorado Rockies, the same mountains to which my former self traveled from Missouri to spend every possible summer in a family mountain cabin. Knowing this confirmed my lifelong desire to explore that area.

Then this life's plan moved me on. One summer evening, I received a vision that shifted my whole reality within one-half hour. Three weeks from receiving new "orders," I had sold everything and arrived at my next location, New York City.

## HAPPY TRAILS

*The following story shows how a thread from a past-life connection can become woven into a present-life tapestry, creating a strong pull to unconsciously reenact aspects of the past scenario in order to progress beyond it. It is a lovely reminder of the connection two souls can have beyond lifetimes and of how the heart-link spurs the evolution of both.*

Hal, my husband of twenty-three years, was retired from the railroad. I was a retired nurse, drawing a small pension from the state. I owned a successful business. Life was good but very busy for me. Hal had the time he had always dreamed of to enjoy family functions, play his harmonica or just read and nap. He had worked hard all his life. Aside from his daily hikes of five or six miles, he enjoyed taking it easy.

Hal began to talk about what I should do if anything happened to him. He would tell me to find another husband if he should pass on, so I wouldn't be lonely. This kind of talk scared me. I wondered if he was holding something back. He denied that he was having trouble, simply saying that he knew he would die first. He went for a full battery of tests, which all came back negative. I still had a nagging feeling that he knew something no one else knew and that he would die soon, leaving me alone. He just didn't know how or why he knew this.

I respected what he was telling me, so I spent more time with him, watching him closely. Leaving my business in good hands, we set out to enjoy all the things we had always wanted to do, things we had never done because there was never enough time. We took a cruise. With a couple of our children we flew to Costa Rica, where Hal enjoyed using his second language. We drove our motor home from California to Florida. We created some wonderful memories.

Hal never revealed any symptoms of illness. His typically excellent blood pressure remained that way. He did not seem depressed, but continued to feel overwhelming sadness about leaving me. He never seemed to be afraid of dying. It was the thought of our parting that caused him so much sorrow.

Trusting his feelings, I began to share his impressions of my being without him. Whenever I was home alone, it felt very strange, as if there were something to which I was supposed to pay attention. When I sat still for long periods, an overwhelming sense of grief and loss would come over me. My heart felt as if it were breaking. I was content to sit by his side, even while he was napping. I would sit and watch him. I studied the shape of his head, the way the skin lay across his cheeks. I felt very nurturing toward him, calling him, "My boy, my sweet boy." I think I was trying to burn the vision of him into my memory. I also could no longer deny the feeling that I would be losing him soon.

Hal and I had become much more spiritual, even though he was angry with God, knowing for certain that he would be leaving me alone. But not once did he express a fear of dying.

During those eighteen months, we had the closest, sweetest relationship I could ever have imagined. We waited on each other, bringing little treats to serve with tea or wine. We would sit in a perfect little romantic spot in the garden, tucked into our five acres, or sit for hours on the patio. Now it feels like a wonderful dream.

Hal cried every night, however, afraid that he would not wake up. We held each other and tried to let it go, knowing that we really could not change what we felt was inevitable. We also knew that we couldn't love each other more.

When his time came, we were sitting in church, with our son and his family, in another town. Hal sat beside me, our hands less than six inches apart. I turned to smile at him and saw his head roll back. His eyes looked blank. Three doctors from the congregation did CPR. He was gone in an instant, like a candle that had been snuffed out.

Oh, my God, not here, not now! I thought. I wanted to say one last good-bye. I heard the church choir singing in the background while I watched them try to resuscitate Hal. Their efforts were futile.

I stepped away from the others for a moment. It was then that I felt a shift. I turned to my son and his wife, saying, "Something is happening!" I could hear no sounds. Up and to the right of those who were huddled over his body, I suddenly saw a slight wisp, like a light puff of smoke. I watched in amazement as it moved to my chest in an instant flash. It took my breath away. I said, "He's here! He's right here! Now! With me!" Then I had no need to know the outcome. I didn't care to ride in the ambulance with his body. I knew that he was with me. I felt calm. I helped decide on transportation to the hospital, even though I knew that it was futile. I wanted them to leave his poor body alone.

My son was in shock, so someone else had to drive us to the hospital. Tears fell with the realization of what had just happened. I thought about the first time that I had stepped into that church. It was several months before, right after my son and his family moved to Modesto. Patti, my daughter-in-law, and I had just dropped the children off at their Sunday school classes. We hurried to the main chapel, entering from the same outer breezeway.

We crossed the short lobby and quickly went up the stairs to sit in the balcony. When I heard the choir open in beautiful harmony, an overwhelming wave of sadness and sorrow had come over me. I stepped back as tears flooded. I sobbed, not knowing why, and I clung to the wall. Patti walked back to see where I'd gone. I could not explain what was happening to me.

Now I knew I had experienced a future moment when I would sit with Hal for the last time. Everything felt surreal, as if I were just a character in a play, moving through my life, thinking that I was doing my own thing. All the while, there seemed to have been a master plan that had nothing to do with my choices.

We were ushered into a private waiting room right next to the emergency room. Church and hospital people came and went, trying to give us hope. I felt confused. I knew that Hal was dead, that nothing they could do in the ER could make a difference. I knew that he was not there. He was here, sitting beside me. I wanted to be alone. I wanted to wake up from this nightmare.

It was calming for me to replay a scene from the night before. Hal and I were preparing for bed in our motor home. We had attended a wedding that day, and planned to attend church with our kids the next morning. I had felt a sudden wave of terrible foreboding. I cried for several hours not wanting to face the morning. I didn't understand my feelings, I just wanted to run away from tomorrow. Hal could not console me, and eventually drifted off to sleep, holding me in his arms. Now I understood what the feeling had meant.

A couple of months later, experiencing deep, deep grief, I would sit and try to accept that Hal was gone. I was left with many years ahead to be spent apart, while still feeling his presence. It was a torturing pain that reminded me of my need for him. Sometimes, when I realized that he could not come back to life, I entertained thoughts of joining him. More and more frequently, I would awaken in the night in tears, feeling totally absorbed by his presence. How was I going to help myself?

The answer came, strangely enough, from Hal. One day, my youngest daughter invited me to stay for dinner. Afterward, my two grandchildren moved to the living room to watch a TV program. Lori asked how I was doing. She sounded like she really wanted to know. Immediately I burst into tears. I told her that I did not know how I would survive Hal's death. I wasn't sure that I wanted to survive. Lori moved her chair closer to me, leaning across the corner of the table to put her arms around me.

She said that she'd had a dream. "Pop" came to her, saying that I was at risk and that I could not come where he was! She said that even though I was right there next to him in the dream, I could not hear him say this. He repeated the message several times, emphasizing how seriously I was at risk. "My God!" I said. I was stunned at what she said. I stopped crying, instantly. My daughter continued to talk. She reassured me of all the reasons I was needed and loved. She made me promise not to think of anything as terrible as suicide. She insisted that I stay the night.

I couldn't sleep, but I must have, because I was suddenly jerked awake by a terrible disturbance in my chest. I knew from my experience as a nurse that my heart was in atrial fibrillation! The upper chamber of my heart was beating in an erratic fast pace, while the main lower chamber continued to pump, though stressed, to move the blood throughout my body.

I tried everything to calm myself. I tried changing my position. I went into the living room, so I could sit straight up, hoping the full change of position would convert the rhythm. Nothing helped. I began to think about dying, about taking advantage of being in a very precarious medical state. I was confused about what Lori's dream was really saying.

I didn't want to disturb my daughter's family. They all had a busy schedule the next day. So I drove myself home. I reasoned that there would be less traffic in the middle of the night, driving into the foothills. Fortunately, I was right. My decision did not jeopardize anyone else's safety.

The cardiac disturbance continued. By the time I reached home thirty minutes later, my heart was tired. I didn't know for sure if the dream meant that if I killed myself, I would not get to go where Hal was. Or did it mean that even if I died naturally, I still could not go where he was, because my life had not been good enough? I was tormented, trying to understand what the dream meant.

Three and one-half hours had passed, my chest rocking like a washing machine out of balance. I called the advice nurse at my HMO, when my heart returned to a normal beat! I hung up the phone, hearing her urge me to call 911. I felt a wonderful sense of peace and knew that it was more than a release from the arrhythmia. I felt clear. I had just made a decision to live.

I said, "Thank you," and drifted off to sleep on the couch as the sun came up. When I awoke that morning, I felt like I was beginning a new chapter in my life. I thought to myself, If this is the way it's going to be, then I want to do my part to understand this. I want to thrive!

I bought books dealing with life after death, about how the spirit continues beyond death. I began to meditate, which helped me focus and quiet myself. I attended the Monroe Institute in Virginia, which taught me to experience my astral body, which travels in and out of my physical body. But even with these helpful experiences and many more books, I felt myself starting to slip back into hopeless sorrow. I needed some answers.

When I did the dishes, one of Hal's chores, I often heard myself singing or humming the old Roy Rogers song "Happy Trails to You . . ." I kept wondering why we had known that he would die.

One night I decided at the last moment to attend a talk, given by Louise Hauck, at the local Learning Exchange. As soon as she began to speak, I felt tremendous peace. I listened intently to every word she spoke. At the end we were told only three appointments remained for personal consultations. I got scheduled, in spite of the crowd that stood in line. I was ecstatic. I counted the days until our meeting!

What a life-changing experience it turned out to be. I got some of the sweetest words of confirmation from Hal, through Louise. Her words could only have come from Hal. He was talking about things that had happened in those moments when I was alone, feeling his presence.

I also learned my father, mother, brother and grandparents—who had already passed over—could not wait to prove it was really they. They sent me their loving thoughts. Louise told me of many more things that would be coming into my life as a result of this life-changing event—losing Hal—as if it were meant to be. Louise ended with a little song from all of them on the Other Side: "Happy Trails to You . . ."

At last, I had some answers. My experiences had been validated. I was not losing my mind. Now I could move forward and reach out to others for help. I started my own bereavement group for widows. I found that there were many of us who needed more than learning about the various stages of grief.

Louise was interested in finding out why Hal and I were given, in advance, the information and awareness about his departure. She came to speak to my bereavement group that had grown during this time. She stayed a few days to do private consultations. During that week, Louise gave me another reading, where she was able to access the information we had been looking for.

It involved one of a few other incarnations that Hal and I had shared. Louise described an "overlay" where she saw me in a dark and dreary scene, locked in a prison cell, fearful and overwhelmed. I was sitting at the bedside of my critically ill young son. It was Hal. It all sounded as if right out of a Charles Dickens novel. Louise saw details, such as the suspenders that my son wore. Apparently I was unable to get the medical care needed to save his life. Our desperation drew us together with a determination and love to help each other by remembering to feel God's light and to trust God's plan. Louise said that I sat with my son for weeks and months, watching over my boy, "my sweet boy."

As I listened, I recognized the same feeling I used to have when I watched Hal sleep, all those many months before his passing. Sending my heartfelt love and desperate prayers to keep him with me also felt very familiar. Louise described how the bond that had developed over lifetimes was in place, drawing us together again, creating a new potential.

For what purpose? I was thinking. Only to be torn apart again? Immediately Hal gave Louise a direct answer to my silent query! He said that because we had developed such a deep connection over lifetimes, and because I had grieved well and grown from my search for truth and understanding in the aftermath of our most recent experience, we are now able to take our loving connection to a higher, eternal level. We had survived our greatest hurdle. We could now proceed with some very important work, together.

Hal emphasized that with his support—and that of my parents on the Other Side—my intuitive awareness will increase, allowing me to assist others in their search for meaning in life after loss. He said how proud he was of me. He knew that I was more comfortable now, able to sense his eternal self, rather than the Hal I remembered. He knew that I felt less pain over the loss of his physical form, allowing a richer and healthier foundation to emerge. I sensed that in losing the love of my life, new and wonderful doors were opening. I could look forward to new adventures. And Hal and I would maintain a connection that would benefit both of our spiritual paths.

It has been just one year as I write this. My family and friends are amazed that I have done so well. I am, too! My life after Hal's death is a testimony to the realization that we live in a multidimensional world. And we receive the blessings of this life when we embrace it fully and trust our God-given gifts.

*Jan Pikowsky*

## THE STAR-SHAPED BALLOON

*This account comes from Don, a man who did not think he would survive the loss of his wife, Jackie. We discovered that there was a momentum toward self-destruction that had begun in a previous life and threatened to destroy this one.*

*In the first sessions, Jackie presented an entertaining assortment of evidence that included specific memories from the past. She named different animals that she and Don had loved and cared for over the years, showing me scenes of her horse, Star, and Gigi, the guinea pig. One session began with Jackie showing me—pantomime fashion—a scene that I interpreted as someone placing a baking sheet of cookies in the oven.*

*"Was Jackie very domestic? Did she bake cookies?" I asked.*

*"No," Don replied quickly, "she was not at all domestic. She rarely baked anything." The next morning, I picked up this phone message from Don: "Hello, Louise. Do you remember in my consultation yesterday, when you saw that my guinea pig, Gigi, had died? Well, I had the body cremated and buried it near the plot reserved for Jackie and me. This morning I called the vet to ask how he cremated Gigi's body. He said, 'Well, it's kind of like putting the body on a cookie sheet, then we slide it in the*

oven.' Jackie was telling us that she knows all about Gigi!"
Whaddayaknow! I thought to myself. I never know what kind of
confirmation will be meaningful to a client.

The last time Don had a consultation, he cried out to Jackie,
"Louise says that if I can move through this pain, that there
will be gifts to receive. I WANT TO KNOW WHAT THE
GIFTS ARE!"

It's as if Jackie had become impatient with Don's inability to
move on to new adventures and experiences in his life. She herself was currently moving to new levels (frequencies) as a result
of her learning on the Other Side.

She replied, emphatically, "You are LIVING the GIFT! You
have been given the gift of another lifetime in which to learn to
value the precious gift of your LIFE!"

In that moment I viewed an overlay of a past life which
revealed that Don had lost Jackie before and did commit suicide
by drinking himself to death. I saw him stumbling down an
alley, having become miserable, bitter and mean. I could see that
there had been a daughter-in-law who tried to help him, but he
turned her away with his mean words and deeds.

"I've turned away my own daughter, this lifetime," Don
commented, softly.

Don believed that God had let him down, taken his wife
and abandoned him. Fortunately—according to plan—the
pain of his loss forced him to ask some very important questions
about life, death and his own personal journey. Had he not
experienced the pain of such a loss, Don might not have been
attentive to his life's plan and the new signs set in place to lead
him down new avenues. By now, Don has come to see his life
from the perspective of the bigger picture, and has chosen to

*remain on his path on earth this lifetime until his learning and lessons are complete.*

My life is separated into two distinct segments—before March 18, 1995, and after March 18, 1995. Before March 18, 1995, I was on a horizontal path of materialism, not on a vertical path to God. I am an educated person with one technical school degree and three college degrees. My wife, Jackie, was a successful Ph.D.-level psychologist in private practice and I was an architect/administrator. We were amassing material wealth beyond the dreams of most people who are entrenched in the material preoccupation.

Jackie was an energetic person who exercised four to five days a week, ate healthy foods, took vitamins and ran about eight miles a day. She was forty-nine years old, but actually she appeared to be much younger because of her beauty and her health. One day she became ill with the flu. Two days later, on my birthday, she was dead.

Four major operations were performed in the attempt to save her life, all to no avail. The doctor said that the flu virus had attacked her heart and there was no effective treatment. Life-support systems had to be turned off and I watched the person with whom I had lived for twenty-eight years and nine months—the only person that I truly loved unconditionally, the only person that I would have gladly died a million agonizing deaths for—slowly die before my eyes.

I could not eat for weeks and I could not sleep without medication for months. I had reached the point of planning to kill myself using carbon monoxide.

One day after I had purchased the equipment to perform the deed, one of my friends asked me to go to an "intuitive" who was in town for only a few days. My friend said that she had just come from her seminar and that she might be able to help me. This intuitive's name was Louise Hauck.

I was not spiritual at all and had only a vague idea of what an intuitive was. At that point I was so depressed that nothing mattered, so I made the appointment and went on May 9, 1995, to see Louise. I expected to be greeted by a woman in gypsy clothes sitting in front of a crystal ball. Quite conversely, I was met by a beautiful person, her hair up on her head and wearing business clothes. Nothing in the room resembled a crystal ball.

Louise gave me a warm hug and we sat facing each other over a coffee table. She began her prayer to God to let only the information come through for the highest good of all. I thought it was a bit strange to bring God into the scene, but my thoughts were, What the hell, I haven't seen anybody pray for decades and it could be sort of interesting. I knew that there was probably a God out there somewhere, but I didn't particularly connect it to anything happening in my present life. I didn't see why Louise should be asking God anything.

At that one-hour meeting I was blown off my feet. Louise told me things that I knew for a fact only Jackie and I knew. She even described Jackie's features and the clothes Jackie owned. Louise said that Jackie was telling her that I was planning on committing suicide. Jackie added that I had committed suicide under similar circumstances in another life. It would certainly be my choice this time also; however, if I did I would be sleeping a long time in the same place that I did the last time I committed suicide.

She said that God had given me another chance to live through the same circumstances again and again until I worked through the pain of her death. I was bewildered and confused. How did Louise know that I was planning to commit suicide? I had told no one, not even my closest friends. I thought that she might be reading my mind. I had heard of people who could do this, but I had never met one.

I came up with an idea. I told Louise if Jackie was really there, have her predict something that was going to happen to me in the near future. I thought if it were in the future, it would not be in my mind at that time, so it would not register for her to read. However, if it were to come true, I would have to believe her.

Jackie said through Louise, "Okay, you will know that I am with you when this happens: You will be at a meeting. There will be a speaker at the podium and a glass of water close by. Something will happen and the person at the podium will stop his speech, make a joke about it, and the audience will laugh."

Jackie was very involved with her professional career and very active in professional organizations. I was to be presented with a memorial plaque commemorating her by one of the organizations on May 21, about two weeks after my May 9 session with Louise. I thought if this crazy prediction were to take place, it had to be at that meeting. I told some of my friends about it, to see if it really would happen as predicted.

On May 13, several of my friends accompanied me to a seminar at the University of Maryland sponsored by the Association for Research and Enlightenment (Edgar Cayce's group) and featuring guest speakers Rob Grant and Dannion Brinkley. My mind had decided that the prediction would occur at the memorial plaque meeting, not this seminar.

Rob Grant was at the podium speaking to a large audience about his recently published book, *Are We Listening to the Angels?* The title itself, I realized later, must be an interesting message from Jackie. All of a sudden, a star-shaped silver plastic balloon appeared from seemingly nowhere, floating out through a twelve-inch slit in the backstage curtain and the wall on Rob's far-left side. Interestingly enough, Jackie had owned a horse, which she dearly loved, named Star. I buried her with a lock of Star's mane in her hand.

The balloon did not sway up or down, but came straight across the back curtain for about thirty feet in a direct line—at eye level—as though someone were carrying it. When it reached a point, directly behind Rob, it stopped over a pitcher and glass of water next to the curtain. Then it approached Rob and brushed him on his head.

Rob ducked, stopped his speech, then commented, "Well, there must be angels with us today." The audience roared. The balloon proceeded out toward the group and landed in one of the few empty seats, next to a woman in the center of the audience.

I later learned that this woman is a psychologist with a Ph.D., possibly the only psychologist at the meeting. I eventually got to know this person through very unusual circumstances. She said she knew at the time that there was more to this story than we might imagine, and she knew she would learn the whole truth someday. The person beside her hit the balloon back into the air and it floated back to the stage and hovered over the glass of water until the end of the seminar.

At the next session with Louise, Jackie asked me how I liked the balloon show. I said it was great, but I asked, "How did she do that?" She said she had the help of many spirits. At one of the sessions with Louise, Jackie thanked me for putting yellow flowers on her grave only one hour before the session. I know that Louise knew nothing about that until Jackie told her at the session. It was the only time I had ever gone to her grave.

My life before Jackie's so-called death was interesting, but my life since her death has been fascinating. I have read more than 250 books on spirituality and on the near-death experience. I asked Jackie at one of my many sessions with Louise why she died on my birthday. She said to help turn me around and get me on the path to God.

Jackie said that we could work together more efficiently and effectively to help others, with her on the Other Side. I was told that I would pass over when I'm very old. My goal for the rest of my life will be devoted to working for God and helping people.

I have learned over the past three years that there is nothing but love, or the lack of love, which is fear. We are on earth to love, to help other people and to learn through experience. Beyond that, nothing else matters. It's unimportant—what kind of clothes I wear, the kind of car I drive, or the kind of house I live in. It would take volumes to describe my experiences during the last three years. I have actually seen Jackie's spirit and talked to her in person. I have left my body and been with her in beautiful places where she has taught me wonderful lessons.

Through Louise I learned that I had committed suicide in several other lives, and I almost made the same mistake in this life.

*Don Little*

## Preparation for Becoming a Receiver

Each of the individuals in the stories you've just read found, sometimes very much to their surprise, that they had been in touch with their loved ones. They had, in fact, "received" messages. They simply needed to recognize those moments, to have them validated.

You were born into a world that has taught you to distrust—and even fear—any information that might come to you that cannot be scientifically proven or experienced in a physical way through your five senses. If you are not given a framework or belief system that tells you that it is natural and important for you to receive information intuitively (multisensorily) and that you are capable of perceiving beyond this three-dimensional reality (multidimensionally), then, of course, you may not know that this information exists, much less that you can trust it.

Movies, books, the media and shared personal experiences are exposing the public to new concepts of perception and reality that challenge traditional beliefs. Intuition and spirituality in the workplace are receiving wider coverage in the media. Consultants are training employees to make more intuitive choices, a departure from the old "think-tank" solutions. A new framework is developing. This is how consciousness shifts.

We hear less frequently that events occurring in a seemingly purposeful, well-ordered and synchronized way are "coincidences," that communication from departed loved ones—or telepathy among the physically embodied—is fringe or weird, that making choices based on intuitive or gut-level feelings is irresponsible, or that trusting our own, intimate connection to a Higher Power is arrogant or presumptuous.

Very soon, we will look back on ourselves as having existed in a spiritual vacuum or "dark age," much the way that we look back on a world in which people believed the earth to be flat.

How can you prepare yourself to take part in this awakening of intuitive gifts? At the conclusion of each chapter are sections under the heading "Becoming a Receiver." These will assist you with this process. There are two mandatory things that you must do when you intentionally prepare to receive intuitive information, whether before entering into a meditative state, putting up your antenna to connect with a loved one or preparing to actually read someone.

The first is to begin with an invocation. This invokes the Source and communicates your higher intentions. It can be a simple statement, but it must be from the heart. An apprentice in Jerusalem uses a religious prayer. Here is the personal invocation I recite before each consultation: *As always, I ask that I be a clear facilitator, for the most reliable and relevant information, that is for your highest good to receive, and for my highest good to deliver. I surround us with the Light—for energy, protection and to attract good things. I ask that all the information be within God's sight, according to God's plan for your greater, eternal self.*

Just the act of reciting it takes me deeper. You're welcome to borrow it, modify it, make it your own.

Second, surround yourself with the Light. It's good for protection. You don't want to open yourself up to just anything or any energy that's floating around out there. The Light increases your frequency—ups your amps, so to speak. It helps elevate troublesome issues to a higher level of resolution. Picture a mist of brilliant white Light coming over you, or feel yourself encased in a cylinder of Light, like the one used to "beam up" in the TV series *Star Trek*.

And finally, a word about drugs, medications and mind-altering substances. The range of experiences I present to you came about through each client's—and my own—natural, intrinsic, intuitive abilities and our intimate link to a Higher

Power. One or two apprentices have felt diminished clarity in receiving information while having to take certain prescription medications, such as antidepressants, although they have not been altogether inhibited from "tuning in."

None of my apprentices or clients has reported augmented abilities resulting from smoking marijuana or taking mind-altering substances. I prefer that they do not. One apprentice—a particularly gifted young man—reported much greater clarity in receiving images and symbols in our practice sessions after he had stopped regular use of marijuana.

During a brief stay in Jamaica, a "righteous Rasta"—a practicing Rastafarian as opposed to a "rent-a-dred"—said to me, "There are those who come into this world in the Light. You are one. And there are those who come in darkness. Like myself." He asked about my gifts, and about his own. I told him that he had the potential to bring himself—as well as others—into the Light, and to make a living with the use of his creative talents. Where he felt that smoking "ganja" amplified his connection to "JA" (the Source), I sensed that it prevented greater clarity in understanding the ways that "JA" was attempting to guide him to make more illuminating choices in his life.

My host/coordinator in Jamaica was a great fan of a popular musician who had passed over a few years before. I received a message from the singer, who had been trying to reach his family. He wanted my host to know that "there was too much smoke!", implying that certain members of his family had been smoking so much ganja, that he was unable to reach them in their thoughts or dreams.

More recently, I visited an Indian reservation on the East Coast where there is a tradition of using certain substances in religious practices. I also found a very high rate of drug and alcohol abuse there. Spirits of wise teachers appeared quite routinely in consultations that week. One client studies with a medicine man, whose own teacher—now in spirit—confirmed that he had been working with my client on other planes of reality, just as his own student—my client's teacher—was doing with him in the physical dimension. I was only confirming what my client had sensed, through religious practices and teachings on his own spiritual journey.

However, another client, a young woman, was told by a council of elders—now in spirit—that she was meant to be a leader of her peers, an example of living more consciously and intentionally. It was part of her destiny, if her freewill choices would support it, to participate in a future community that would preserve the best of the old ways of her tribe while letting go of the worst of newer influences. In the future, I saw the potential for an emerging perspective (and an actual community) that will not support beliefs in separation or boundaries between her people and the white man, nor with other tribes. Cultural diversity will be preserved. But, she was cautioned, she could participate in that vision and bring forth that Light only by becoming drug free.

## Becoming a Receiver:
## Suspend Your Disbelief and Skepticism

Sensing in an intuitive, multisensory way is simply different from the way most of us were taught to interpret sensory information in our world. Skeptics, as we will see in chapter 7, diminish their own abilities with their continual attempts to disprove intuition by trying to fit nonphysical phenomena into one system or another to which it doesn't relate. Attempting to define intuitive sensing in scientific terms is like trying to measure the velocity of an impulse. You can leapfrog over tedious doubt that retards your multisensing growth when you stop trying to prove this new kind of reception through your rational mind. The information you will receive is not rational—but it exists.

## TRY THIS

Write down the fears you may have about opening up to a new way of perceiving. Think about the things you learned to fear or to doubt throughout your childhood. Did your family project fear about ideas that were new or different? Think of instances in the past where you formed judgments about ideas that simply differed from your way of thinking and later, with increased familiarity, you may have revised those impressions. You may have also formed judgments about people who believe differently from you, or whose customs seem unusual. Was there ever such an instance when your perceptions changed once you got to know them?

CHAPTER TWO

# Sudden Deaths

*S*ome of my clients have lost loved ones in very unexpected, dramatic and sometimes violent ways. They may still be in shock when we first meet, angry at God and possibly thinking of ending their own lives. Still, their loss, however painful, can be their awakening. Their devastation leads them to ask some important questions about God—or a Higher Power—and about life and death. And frequently, they are surprised to receive answers from a Source that is extremely responsive.

Unmistakable road signs in the form of amazing synchronicities—the right book or teacher appearing out of nowhere—or the sense that there is a plan, a bigger picture, allow them to feel increasingly embraced, watched over and guided by "the Source."

This isn't to say that new insights erase anyone's pain. I can only relate to my clients' pain from where I have experienced my own—through the loss of parents and other friends and family. For me, it has taken years for that "scooped out" feeling to transform into more peaceful reflection.

I can't imagine the pain that some of my clients live with, following the sudden loss of a child or a beloved spouse. That is why I feel so blessed to be able to deliver messages from souls, now in the nonphysical dimension, who occasionally allow me to move into their consciousness to experience exactly what they experienced at the time they left their physical bodies.

## THE VALUEJET CRASH

*This first report comes from the mother of "Jay." I was just about to address a large audience on a "Dreamtime Cruise." I was waiting at the podium for everyone to find their seats. Before the room was even one-fourth full, I felt the presence of a soul to my right. I sensed that he had been a young man who had died in a plane crash. I also felt the letter "J" around him.*

*"Just a sec!" I said to the "J" soul, telepathically. "You'll have to wait a moment, for everyone to be seated."*

*Sure enough, both of "J's" parents found seats directly in front of me, in the front row. When all the seats were filled and everyone was quiet, I short-stopped my routine introduction and immediately reported the "visit" to the audience. The couple who sat before me confirmed that their son's nickname was Jay. He had died in the ValueJet crash in the Florida Everglades. I had never met the couple, nor did I realize their connection to "J" until they raised their hands.*

*I relayed that he was doing fine, looking radiant and happy.*

*"I've finally found my MISSION," he said to his parents. Susan, Jay's mother, said that he often said that he longed to know his special mission in life.*

*I continued, "It seems that Jay knows that his sister has dated two young men at the same time. He also knows that she has pierced her ears twice." Jay went on to mention a friend with an "M"—a Matt, Mike or Mark—who he knows to be in a lot of pain as a result of the accident. Jay said, "Tell him that I'm fine," and then he reminisced about how they used to drink some beverage and laugh so hard that it bubbled out their noses.*

*Then I said that Jay had helped another soul to the Light— a name with two double letters in the middle, like "Anna"—and that there was the color of yellow around them before they left their bodies. This information got confirmed in very interesting and unexpected ways, which Susan reported back to me. Here is her story.*

We have begun a quest that we never dreamed we would commence. We would trade it and all we possess if we could have our precious, most wonderful son back with us. He was killed on May 11, 1996, in the ValueJet airline crash. He was just twenty-four years old.

In January 1998, my husband, Paul, and I took a special cruise. It was our first, and the theme was "The Inner Voyage." Paul was reluctant because spirituality—other than traditional Christian religion—was unfamiliar to him. We attended a presentation given by Louise Hauck the third evening of the cruise.

When we entered the meeting room, I led Paul up to the front row. He asked me why we had to sit so close and quipped, "Are we going to be part of a show or something?" I answered that I just wanted to be able to see and hear everything clearly. I was on a mission to learn everything I could about this new subject that I felt compelled to explore since Jay's tragic death.

Louise began to speak, relating her background and how she began her "career" as a seer. A short while into her presentation she mentioned that there was someone from the "Other Side" who was anxious to come through. She politely addressed the individual and asked if he/she would be patient. She then continued speaking to the audience, but very shortly turned and said that the person was excited about getting through. She asked if anyone in the room had lost a child in a plane crash.

We were the only ones to acknowledge by raising our hands. She then asked if the letter "J" meant anything to us. Our son's nickname is Jay. Louise related that Jay said he was very proud of us. Then she asked if the letter "M" had any significance. I thought of my daughter's husband and Paul thought of Jay's fellow officer/supervisor. Louise said she "saw" people laughing after drinking something and the people laughed so hard that liquid came through their noses. We thought that was odd, but Jay had a very quick, dry humor and would so often take people by surprise.

We were anxious to get off the ship at San Juan, Puerto Rico, to call our daughter to ask if she could recollect any of the incidents that Louise described. Our daughter confirmed that the first situation she described fit for both of the Michaels who had come to mind! Louise also added that an "M" person had been having bad dreams and she wondered if this related to Jay's death in the plane crash. Our daughter confirmed that it was our son-in-law who was having the nightmares, though they were about putting his knee back together after recent critical surgery.

She confirmed all of this when we spoke with her from San Juan. She also confessed that before her marriage, she had been dating two men at the same time. We already knew that she had double-pierced her ears!

Louise told us she saw a fort. Paul was an Air Force officer and had been stationed in Manhattan, New York. We lived at Fort Hamilton, Brooklyn, when Jay was born. She said she saw lots of flags and wondered if Jay was in a flag corps, though she didn't say American flags. We assumed that she was seeing that we always put American flags around Jay's monument at the cemetery near our home. But we have also received five full-size American flags from military units in honor and memory of Jay. He was a very patriotic second lieutenant in the U.S. Air Force and was looking forward to becoming a first lieutenant. On July 1, 1996, they promoted him posthumously.

At a subsequent session aboard the cruise, Louise informed us that just before she fell asleep that first night, Jay had thanked her for allowing him to come through to us. She said that it was unusual for that to happen. My husband and I commented, "That would be just like Jay. An officer and a gentleman." Always so polite.

Louise was puzzled that Jay sensed that he had not been fearful at the time of the crash. We could only reply that it must have been because he thought the plane would land. The plane had leveled at approximately four hundred feet after a steep dive. Then the nose went down and the plane "disappeared" into the Everglades.

Louise asked if Jay knew any of the other passengers. He was communicating about a person he knew on the plane. She said the person had double letters in the name and she gave the example of "Bill" or "Ann" as a name with double letters. We answered, "No, he made the brief two-night trip to Miami alone in order to commission his fraternity little brother. He wanted to get home on Saturday to be with us for Mother's Day. If only he wasn't always SO THOUGHTFUL!" "Well," Louise continued, "it seems that Jay helped this person to the Light!"

Louise stated that Jay was carrying something under his arm and she asked if the color yellow had any significance. We could only guess that it might be a gift, but knew he would not have had the time or transportation to shop the short time he was away. Then Louise talked about ropes or cables and asked if we knew how they might be related.

We could only guess that she was referring to the horrific, difficult recovery of remains and wreckage following the crash in the murky swamp. We left that session with so many questions that could not be answered, but so grateful that Jay was keeping "in touch" with us. We miss him more than words can describe.

On March 17, 1998, Paul and I traveled to Miami to participate in the dedication of a memorial to five of the ValueJet victims who were associated with the University of Miami. Jay had graduated in May 1994. Two other mothers and I spoke at the ceremony. The ceremony was a moving experience for everyone attending. Following the ceremony, a reception was held at a professor's residence. As the reception came to a close, the mother of a victim—a nineteen-year-old girl—approached me.

The mother informed me that she had met with John Edward, a psychic who resides in New York, in October of 1997. The session took place in her hometown of New Orleans. He told her that her daughter had been scared when trouble occurred aboard the plane. He said, "Jay took her by the arm and took her into the Light and she was not afraid." This young lady's name was Ana. This was the name that Louise had related to us, without the "double letter" spelling.

We learned that Ana was dating one of Jay's fraternity brothers and had arrived at the airport early the day of the flight, as Jay had. The flight was delayed in boarding because the plane had experienced electrical problems during the flight from Atlanta to Miami. There was no assigned seating, so everyone could sit wherever they wanted.

Jay, we feel sure, was wearing the yellow shirt with his fraternity and the University of Miami logos on it. Since Jay, Ana and another young UM student were such extroverts, they no doubt began a conversation and sat together on the plane. They may have found each other, recognizing the yellow school T-shirts.

One of my prayers just after the crash was to know whom Jay sat with. I had wanted to meet the family of the person whom Jay may have comforted, or who may have comforted Jay. Then Louise mentioned that Jay had helped another to the Light. I felt my prayer had been answered.

Ana's mother told us that John Edward related that Jay had been standing up trying to open the compartment above their heads that held the oxygen masks. He felt that he was trying to use a key or sharp object. We had learned from the cockpit voice recorder transcript that a flight attendant had been screaming, "We need oxygen back here!" But the masks would not release, since they are only for depressurization, not for smoke and fire. There is no protection on a commercial aircraft for smoke and fire.

We also learned that Ana's favorite color was yellow. We wondered if that was relative to the yellow Louise had mentioned to us. Ana's mother seemed timid about telling me of her meeting with John Edward, but we were so grateful that she shared the information with us. It meshed so beautifully with the information Louise had related. We are grateful that Louise has the courage to share her gift and we feel fortunate that we have had the opportunity to meet with her.

It is not the natural order of things that a bright, kind, loving, caring child be senselessly and tragically killed. Our grief has set us on a spiritual path searching for any assurance and evidence that life does continue after death, exploring whether there is a way to communicate. We welcome this search, despite the skepticism or criticism of others who have not traveled our path. Our faith assures us that we will someday again be united with our most wonderful son.

*Susan Smith*

Some people believe that communication with the "deceased" can delay them—detaining them on their path—and even keep them earthbound, when they ought to be moving forward on their soul's journey. I have found that there are many souls on the Other Side who remain in a sort of cocoon state, unable to progress until they have the opportunity to connect—to communicate—with a loved one. Such communication can actually further the growth of loved ones on both sides.

Statements in consultations from loved ones on the Other Side confirm the positive effects from being in communication. These are just two examples.

Rose often experienced an awareness of her deceased husband while she slept. It felt so real to her that she would awaken in the morning, weeping from the realization that he no longer lay beside her in their bed. In the consultation, he was trying to confirm her sensing that she was often with him, that they had been doing many things together on the astral plane. He reported that she was joining him at night in her astral (etheric, nonphysical) body. He looks forward to working together in the future on projects that would allow him to transmit information. He will help "coach" her in helping others to not fear death.

He said, "When you've moved through the grief that comes from missing the physical me, then you'll begin to know the eternal me. We can look forward to working together from both sides!"

Tina had lost her husband three years prior to attending a talk that I gave at her local bookstore. I had to raise my voice to be heard over her sobbing in the back row. The bookstore owner kindly handed her a box of Kleenex. She used nearly the entire box by the time I concluded my presentation. A few days later when she came for a personal consultation, her husband—a cowboy in his physical life with her—offered in a kind and gentle manner, "You don't need to hold on to the pain, to hold on to me!"

## BOMBING IN JERUSALEM

*There is a kind of holding on to a loved one that is not beneficial for the survivor nor for the deceased soul. It might be helpful to picture a wife kissing a child or husband as they prepare to go off to school or to work, or a parent hugging his/her child good-bye as he/she departs for an evening out, leaving the child at home with the baby-sitter.*

*As they start to leave through the opened door, the wife—or the child—becomes engulfed with fears and tugs frantically at the child/husband/parent. The one left behind is inconsolable, unable to let go. The one who leaves cannot do so freely nor happily, feeling pulled back by the one who holds on in despair. It's the same effect when we lose a loved one and become stuck in our never-ending grief. New adventures don't tempt with new choices, and the passage of time does nothing to help the healing process. Life becomes static. The consuming focus is on the void left by the one who has departed.*

*I have consulted for countless clients who are healing from devastating losses. I've experienced only a few who might have jeopardized a loved one's journey after "death" by refusing to let their grief transform in life-expanding, life-affirming ways.*

*In the following story, a grieving wife feared that she had detained her husband from going to the Light. For weeks she sat at his bedside, pleading and begging for him not to leave her. He lay in a coma, his body burned and both legs amputated from the ghastly bombing of the bus he had boarded in Jerusalem. I had read about terrorist bombings such as this, but did not know specifically about this one that had occurred months before my arrival in Israel. It took place not too far from where I was staying. I had never met this client before our first session, nor was I aware of the circumstances surrounding her loss. I was unaware that she had even experienced a loss.*

*Each time that I have consulted for Shoshanna, her husband comes through exceptionally loud and clear. I can only surmise why some souls "transmit" more clearly and with greater exuberance than others. Factors may involve (a) the degree to which the soul is progressing on its journey since making the transition from the physical dimension, (b) the receptivity of my client to connecting with the deceased, and (c) one and/or the other's receptivity—or hesitancy—toward looking at their path's configuration from a new perspective. Or it may simply be a matter of how adept a soul is in finding the right frequency—tuning in to the right station—to transmit.*

*In this case, my guess is that this soul was extremely grateful for the opportunity to transmit and thereby do some good. There was the potential for him to contribute back to this dimension. It seemed an honor for him to do so, when his less-inspired choices did little to enhance his or anyone else's life while he occupied the body that was taken from him in such an unexpected, violent fashion.*

## The Accident

As usual, my husband awoke, prayed and readied himself to leave for work while I caught another hour or so of sleep. Just before his leaving the house he came to my side of the bed and kissed me on the cheek saying, "I love you." I made no response and pretended to be sound asleep because our relationship at this time was faltering. I thought it a very strange thing for him to do, especially since we were hardly speaking for weeks before.

When I heard the door close behind him, I got out of bed and began my preparations to leave for work. I also awoke my son David for school. It was 6:45 A.M. As usual, I turned the television on and began to watch the morning show *Boker Tov Israel* (Good Morning Israel) while drinking my morning coffee. After hearing the news and weather reports I went about the business of getting dressed.

David was slow this morning. I took the opportunity to have a second cup of coffee and sit and watch the show a few more minutes. Just as David was ready to leave, a news bulletin flashed on the screen. It was 7:40 A.M. It reported a terrorist bus bombing in Jerusalem at about 6:40 A.M.

Because of my limited understanding of Hebrew, I asked David to stay and listen and translate. He told me that it happened on Jaffa Road near the bus station. He thought it was bus #36 but wasn't sure.

At this point, as was my habit, I phoned my husband at work to make sure he was there. I was told that he hadn't yet arrived. It was 7:50 A.M. I sent David off to school, but I stayed and listened for more reports. At 8:00 A.M. I again phoned my husband at work. I was told that he still hadn't arrived, but not to worry. There were many traffic jams in town, due to the bombing. I began to shake inside.

I then phoned my son Joseph, who was living in Tel Aviv, and told him about the bombing. I mentioned that I couldn't reach his father. He said he would make some calls and call me back. While I was waiting, I heard them announce on TV that it was bus #18 that was bombed. They began to televise from the scene. My heart raced and again I phoned my husband at work. He was still not there. It was 8:15. I immediately phoned my office.

I work at Hadassah Hospital in the cardiology department. I asked the Hebrew secretary if I heard right about it being bus #18. She said, "Yes," very hesitantly. She knew my husband. Then I asked if she would send one of the doctors down to the emergency room to look for my husband.

She said, "How do you know he was on that bus, and that he didn't take the car?"

I said, "I just have a feeling."

She said, "I'll ask one of the doctors to go down to see. I'll call you back." She was sure that I was worrying unnecessarily.

Meanwhile, Joseph called. He said that he had called the emergency phone number, the one given to families looking for their kin. He said, "Dad's name wasn't on the list."

A close girlfriend phoned to ask if I had spoken with my husband. She had heard about the bombing of bus #18. I told her he hadn't arrived at work. She said, "I'll call you back."

By 8:30 in the morning, I received a call from my office. One of the doctors did go down to the emergency room and did find my husband. I said I would be there as quickly as I could. I then phoned Joseph and told him. He said he would meet me at the hospital as soon as he could get there.

I called my daughter. Her husband told me she hadn't arrived home from the night shift at Hadassah Hospital. She worked in the burn unit. He had already spoken to my son Joseph. He was aware of the situation. We agreed that they would also meet me at the hospital as soon as possible. We decided to leave David in school until we knew more about the situation.

Then I phoned one of my closest friends, who said that she would meet me at Hadassah. Within minutes, there was a knock at the door. Her husband was at the door. I told him that Ira was on the bus that was bombed. He knew. His wife had called him. He drove me to the hospital, where we met his wife. She was anxiously awaiting our arrival.

I phoned upstairs to my office. I asked where I could find my husband. My boss told me that he would come down and take me to him. I felt that I was in slow motion and everything around me was moving at a snail's pace.

My boss arrived and told me that my husband was hurt very badly. He didn't think that I should see him just yet. I insisted, so he took me to the trauma ward. Professor Gotsman, my boss, and Dr. Lotan, the doctor from my department, went to search for my husband. When they found his room, Dr. Lotan and Professor Gotsman escorted me in.

There was my husband, surrounded by nurses, doctors and machines—all working to keep him alive. Dr. Lotan said, "Are you sure you want to see him like this?" Without hesitation I answered, "Yes!"

My husband's legs and hands were all bandaged. His body and face were very swollen, and he had a black eye. I knew he was close to death. The doctors treating him told me that if he survived the next twenty-four hours, he might have a chance.

His lungs were blown from the blast and he was connected to a respirator. To ease the pain, they had anesthetized him. The only part of his body that was functioning on its own was his bladder. They said this was a good sign.

When David arrived, I told him the situation. We comforted each other. Family and friends took up a vigil in the waiting room, praying, hoping and telling stories about times past. The hours turned to days.

Each time I was beside Ira's bed I encouraged him to hold on, to be strong, not to let this terrible thing do him in. We needed him. I would help him with his recovery and be by his side every minute. Days turned into weeks. He had good days (no change in his condition) and bad days (other medical obstacles to overcome).

My husband underwent two emergency surgeries: the first time to open his abdomen in order to reduce the swelling, and the second time for skin grafting on his legs. This was to help fight the infections. When he was stabilized, the doctors stopped the anesthesia, only using intravenous morphine medication. They wanted to see if he would respond. Other than a few grimaces when being shaved, he made no response.

Seven weeks passed. I saw his condition deteriorate. The doctors wanted to amputate his legs. They were the main source of sepsis infection, preventing his body from mending. The antibiotics were no longer working.

I didn't know what to do. I consulted my children. We agreed to the surgery. During the three-hour operation, my children, friends and I sat and prayed. I wanted to believe he would recover, but something told me he wouldn't. He survived the surgery, but when they let me see him, I just knew it was the end.

I stepped back to let the nurses do their job. From there, I said, "Ira you fought a good fight. But I see the end has come. I understand you have to go now." He passed away before the night was over.

In the Jewish religion there are numbers that have special meanings. I am not very learned on this subject. But I was told that, according to the numbers, my husband received the highest honor from G-d, to pass in the seventh week on the forty-ninth day after the bombing. They compare it to the honor of the Jewish people of being given the Torah.

## The Consultation

I was going to have a reading with Louise. I was filled with anxiety, expectation, excitement and reservation. I was also determined not to say very much but to listen and hope to make sense of the experience.

The reading began with family members who had passed on at various times, but then suddenly "Bill" entered the scene waving his arms. I remember first wondering if this could be my husband, Ira, whose middle name was William. Slowly things began to fall in place, and yes, it was my late husband.

To try to describe how I felt at that moment of recognition is difficult. I had so many questions I wanted to ask, things I wanted to say, but he was communicating and all I could do was listen. I was grateful for the tape recording of the session because I played it over and over for the next couple of weeks. It was all so clear to me. He had communicated from the Other Side. It was so like him.

*Shoshanna Weinstein*

*The following is the dialogue that took place in the first consultation with Shoshanna in Jerusalem in 1997. Because of the dramatic details involved in this consultation, I've chosen to share it in a more detailed form. "Bill" appeared right beside me, making it a threesome. I sat facing Shoshanna:*

Louise: "There is one here, whom you would have known as a man, with the name 'Bill.'"

Shoshanna: "Yes. That would be my husband, though Bill was his middle name."

L: "He is so happy, waving his arms about to show you how free he is without the body. Your husband is showing me something about a bus and an explosion."

S: "Yes. He was on the bus that was bombed here in Jerusalem earlier this year."

L: "He's talking about the end. He knows that you have some regrets."

S: "I'm worried that I may have held him back from the Light when I begged him not to leave me and our three children. He was on the trauma ward. I knew he was in a lot of pain, but I couldn't bear to lose him."

L: "Your husband is saying that he heard every word, even while in the coma. He says that you did not hold him back. Quite the contrary. He lingered in order to heal some issues with you. That was being accomplished in those last days, even while you feel that you were holding him back."

S: "I've felt so guilty that . . ."

L: "Now he's saying that he wants to apologize for something . . . some doubts about his fidelity? Was there an issue about this?"

S: "Yes! I had suspected for quite some time that he was having an affair with my best friend. My suspicion has destroyed our friendship. She continues to deny that she had been intimate with my husband."

L: "Bill is sorry that he caused so much trouble and suspicion. He was flirtatious, but not intimate, with your friend. He admits that he often taunted you with his vagueness about important issues. He's not proud that he was such an expert at manipulating people like this. He asks your forgiveness."

S: "Yes. He really made me crazy. I can't tell you how aggravating he could be. I'm so relieved to know. Of course, I forgive him."

L: "He wants your children to know that he's watching over them: The son who plays soccer, the daughter who suffers with multiple sclerosis, the boy with the 'J'—now Bill's showing me a counter with blue combs or brushes."

S: "That would be my son Joe. He's a hairstylist. He recently opened up a new shop. He told me that he was thinking about his dad last week, around the time of the shop opening, wishing that he could know about his success. I believe that the combs and brushes are blue."

L: "He wants Joe to know that he was there. He is so proud of him."

*I told Shoshanna that when she suddenly thinks of Bill—out of the blue, out of context from where her thoughts are going at the time—it's often because he's momentarily connecting with her frequency. He's making a "visit." And sometimes when she has a thought about him, it calls him in. Sometimes it's difficult to discern whose thought has initiated the connection.*

*I mentioned to her about the time when I was speaking to a large audience about how loved ones connect with us. As pure energy, oscillating at a particular frequency—without a body— they come in (or transmit) on the frequency that connects with us instantly. You could say, "They are just a thought away." A woman looked quite perturbed, raising her hand to ask, "Then, do they see everything that we do? Like watching us in the bathroom?"*

*I told her that it's really no different from the times when you are doing something around the house and suddenly think of a friend. Then the friend calls you on the phone. You compare notes, realizing that you had "tuned" in to each other. It is no different in connecting with the frequency of a friend, in or out of the body!*

*I consulted again for Shoshanna in Jerusalem, one year later. Once again, Bill came in crystal clear. This time he had three messages for her.*

*First, Bill allowed me to move into his consciousness to experience what he had felt, just before the death of his body, beyond our perception of linear time. I'm usually happy to do this. Most often I experience that the soul has ejected from the body before impact in sudden deaths, for example, in car and plane crashes, and often, before or at the time of penetration of bullets or knives in murders. (The latter instances involved special cases. I do not choose to tune in to the frequencies involving mayhem.) I do love being able to give evidence that the soul is never killed and, in many cases, that suffering was minimal.*

L: "Bill's saying that at the moment of the bus explosion, he left his body. He thought that he was watching the five o'clock news! Then he realized that it was his body that he saw strewn on the street!"

*I wasn't sure how to communicate Bill's second message. It had something to do with body parts. At first, I assumed that he was still referring to the accident.*

L: "Now Bill is saying, 'While you were worrying about the body parts, I was trying to let you know that I was fine!'"

*Quite often, when I relay messages, I have no idea of their meaning. I simply "give what I get." Sure enough, Shoshanna knew exactly what Bill was referring to.*

S: "Oh, yes! In Judaism, it's forbidden to bury a body that is not whole. I had to ask my son-in-law to go to the hospital to retrieve my husband's legs for the burial. It was quite an ordeal!"

*And finally, Bill sent a lovely memory, showing that the good, the love, the memories are never lost:*

L: "Now Bill is showing me a scene of people in a hotel lobby."
S: "Oh, yes! That was one of our most favorite things to do. We'd pretend that we were staying at a hotel. We would sit in the lobby and watch people!"
L: "He hasn't forgotten. The memory is still with him."

# FATAL JUMP

*Edith suffered a breakdown after the death of her beloved daughter, Stephanie. She scheduled a private session after hearing me speak at the Learning Exchange in Sacramento, less than six months after her loss. After her consultation, I was told that the incident had been in the newspapers, but since I was residing in New York at the time, I was not aware of it.*

*Stephanie fell ten thousand feet to her death in a skydiving accident. She had arranged the adventure for her boyfriend's birthday, the first attempt at skydiving for everyone in her group. Each one had been assigned a "jumpmaster" with whom to jump in tandem, harnessed to each other. Just before she jumped from the plane, she turned to a friend behind her, gave her a thumbs-up, then mouthed, "I love you."*

*It was disclosed by the investigating coroner that Stephanie's partner, a twenty-eight-year-old man, showed traces of marijuana in his body, with a blood alcohol level of 0.04 percent. Even though he was an experienced jumper with more than two thousand jumps, the FAA reported that he never pulled the rip cord to activate the main chute.*

*I experienced that Stephanie—in her etheric body—had somersaulted out of her physical body shortly after making the jump, even before it fell halfway to the ground. There was a brief sensation of frustration, feeling tangled cords around her legs. Then it felt like she was almost "yanked" out of the body. She hovered around her body for a short time—made the connection that she was no longer in it—then was pulled to the Light.*

In deep depression, Edith longed for a dream that would give her evidence that a connection to her daughter still existed, but nothing happened. Our session confirmed that her daughter had been reaching her mother all along, but in her own way.

Initial confirmation from Stephanie came in the form of friends' names. She mentioned one name with an "S," and then projected a scene of someone drawing pictures in the sand. Then the name "Rosa."

"That's the friend with whom she had recently traveled to South Africa," said Edith. The girl later confirmed that that's where Stephanie had drawn pictures in the sand. This same friend also mentioned that she had driven to Santa Rosa one day, shortly after Stephanie's passing. She felt Stephanie stroke her hand. At that moment, she knew that she was with her. In the consultation, Stephanie was simply confirming that she had made a momentary visit.

Then Stephanie gave me the initials of her boyfriend. "She's saying that this younger man is looking up to you for guidance. He is gaining insights from you." A very compassionate young woman in life, Stephanie was now continuing in her caring manner. I added, "He is able to perceive things in a nonphysical way." I encouraged her to tell him that he can trust those sensings. Later he confided to Edith that he had experienced contact with Stephanie—twice.

Then I tried to decipher the next picture I received—of a Bundt cake. Edith said, "I baked that cake because a feeling came so strongly to me one day—in my heart—that Stephanie wanted for me to bake this cake for her nursing colleagues, where she had worked at a clinic. I just knew!" With that, Stephanie made her famous thumbs-up gesture to me. She continued with more and more scenes, including one of feathers, which signaled the thank-you card decorated with feathers that arrived for Edith a few days later.

So that her mother would learn to trust that her messages would come in different ways, she gave me a few examples: She showed me a caterpillar. Edith mentioned in a note to me that the evening after her session, a caterpillar crawled along the floor in front of the fireplace in her home. Later, three of Stephanie's friends and her father were standing in the garage. Suddenly another caterpillar appeared and crawled past them. While alerting her mother to this kind of "communication," Stephanie also cautioned her mother that she would drive herself crazy if she were to look for signs everywhere!

Stephanie loved music, particularly Sarah McLachlan's "Angel." For months, every time Edith started her car, that was the first song playing on the radio, without fail.

Edith and her husband attend meetings for parents who are struggling to endure the loss of a child. For quite a while, Edith felt terribly sad—and a bit envious—when she heard participants tell of their dreams and spiritual meetings with the children they grieved for. I had told her that the communication would come in simple, unexpected ways. She had only to be open to it coming in on its own—in Stephanie's own way. Now she no longer waits for "the big dream," but takes heart—and gives thanks—for the little ways that she is reminded that her daughter is not so far away. It is in her heart that she finds her confirmation.

## Becoming a Receiver:
## Drop Expectations as to How You Will Receive

In these stories where clients lost loved ones in sudden, very dramatic ways, each one had to let go of how they hoped to be in contact with a lost family member. In spite of their grief, they did not shut themselves off from receiving some form of communication. They all received the evidence they'd prayed for, confirming that their hearts keep them connected and in communication. It was their openness to receive these leads in unexpected ways that brought them their answers.

_____ **TRY THIS** _____

Reflect back on a time when you lost a loved one and longed for some type of confirmation that they were near. Make a list of the kind of ways that you expected to find that evidence. You may have yearned for a very specific type of sign that would give you unmistakable proof. Had your expectations been influenced by others' stories? Did you expect to be shown in very literal ways that would satisfy your rational mind?

If you did receive a response, or what felt like one, how did the ways in which you felt you'd been answered differ from what you expected? Look to see if the evidence you received was much more subtle, or in symbols or images. Your answers come from a dimension—and a Source—that is far more imaginative and creative than your rational mind will ever be!

# CHAPTER THREE

# Reentry: Choosing New Parents

*L*ike so many people with a metaphysical, spiritual perspective, I always accepted the concept that we choose our own parents. I always felt that my life followed an intentional plan that began even before my birth. For me, it was just that—a feeling—but my feeling was confirmed the first time a soul on the Other Side showed me he was coming to this prospective parent—my client who sat before me—and told me why she was chosen.

The soul who hovered around my client in anticipation of his imminent "reentry" said, "I know that you've just moved my crib over to the wall with the blue wallpaper, just across from the window. That's good. I'm going to like light."

Then he added, "And very soon—after my birth—when you see me smile, please know that it won't be 'gas.' I'll truly be smiling up at you." This child-to-be also mentioned how he looked forward to certain influences from his chosen parents. These influences were intended to have a catalytic effect, fostering his soul's growth.

For example, his prospective father tended to be a workaholic, very concerned with making his way to the top in the business world. This ambitious nature resembled a pattern of his own—in another life space—that didn't allow his soul to deepen or his heart to open to family and creative pursuits. This tendency—exhibited in his soon-to-be father—would serve as a sort of backdrop, a reminder of a new focus he is returning to embrace.

When I educate new clients to this perspective—that we choose our parents before birth—they often respond, "Then why did I have to choose *them*?" We don't reenter this dimension to idle in paradise. We come to expand in response to all the ways that life challenges us. And we come, hopefully, to allow the pain to lead us to greater insights about our true nature—who we are and what life is all about.

The magnetic pull that draws our spirit back into this dimension can result from the need for growth, expansion or resolution. Our spirit may be drawn back by the need to balance old choices that have had negative effects on our journey or the need to deliver illuminating gifts that will help our world. Some have brought new technology, inspirational creativity and spiritual enlightenment—these are welcome contributions in this dimension. It's often a combination of all these assorted soul purposes that configure our life's plan and influence the conditions of our reentry to a physical body.

This need for the soul to evolve relates to the obvious question, "Why would a soul—a child—have to come to experience horrific conditions or circumstances, such as starvation,

abuse, even murder?" It is futile to try to understand a soul—
a child—"choosing" to come to those abominable circumstances. In the context of our interpretation of what is good
and what is bad in life, and when viewed from our traditional,
limited perspective, it does not seem to make sense. Why
would a loving God—the Source, a Higher Power—subject
one of its own precious creations to the experience of excruci-
ating pain or early death?

Preparing for a lifetime of growth, rather than one of
"R&R" (rest and reflection), a soul signs up for conditions that
will challenge it and that contain the potential for it to evolve
leaps and bounds beyond any previous life experience. For
example, sacrificing one's life for another is cause for great celebration on the Other Side, when that soul returns "home." It
is a demonstration of faith that defies the illusion of death and
plays out the truth of eternal life.

To live a life in a handicapped or maimed body, coura-
geously transcending pain and physical limitations to discover
deeper gifts and strengths within can raise that soul to greater
heights of understanding. That individual often becomes a
profound teacher by example.

And sometimes, for a myriad of reasons, a soul might vol-
unteer to come to a "shorter tour of duty," an early death. In
some cases, the one who departs awakens those left behind,
prompting them to ask consciousness-changing questions
about life—and death. From a limited perspective, dying early
seems like a bad thing. From an expanded view, that soul gets
to return home, assuming that it was able to accomplish what
it came here to do.

Finally, sometimes there are specific karmic configurations set in motion—or soul agreements made—that would

have the soul experience both sides of an issue. This would, for example, necessitate the murderer in one life space playing the part of the murdered in another; the enslaver, the enslaved; the perpetrator, the victim. I do believe, however, that we are given the opportunity to jump off the "karmic conveyor belt" when we begin to observe from the perspective of the soul, learning and growing from the insights we gain, rather than having to play out a karmic cause-and-effect drama. From the insights come shifts and from these come many gifts.

In consultations, when I spot souls who are preparing to reenter, who seem to be "standing in line" with prospective parents chosen, they appear to me up and to the right of my client's head. They often indicate when and if there has been a useful, challenging or very loving connection forged in a previous incarnation with my client. They communicate what they intend to accomplish in this new life. They often contrast these optimistic images with memories of all that they might not have accomplished during earlier returns.

Occasionally these souls show me objects that are likely to be returned to them—through time and space—in the upcoming journey. They specify incidents that will manifest beyond the suspicion of "coincidence." When they include this information, it always reminds me of the documentaries that demonstrate a tradition in some cultures where religious officials investigate the suspected reincarnation of a lama in Tibet, or a guru in India. They test to see if the child can identify certain objects that belonged to the soul of their previously embodied, beloved leader. Movies have documented the Dali Lama at three or four years old, sorting through an array of objects—jewelry, photos, books, eating implements—and show him going directly to something particular, exclaiming, "This is mine!" He is shown looking at a photo in a book and confirms, "That's me!"

## Children Remembering

I'm witnessing more and more souls these days who indicate to me in consultations that they will be reentering and not needing to forget past-life experiences as most of us have. They do this by pointing to their etheric (as opposed to physical) heads. I often share the story of a woman who, after having a hysterectomy, eventually adopted two children. When the youngest, a little girl, was two years old, she came to her adoptive mother and exclaimed, "I tried to come to you, but there was no room! So I picked a mommy who would know where to find you!"

I did a consultation for a woman in Miami who reported that when her granddaughter was three, she looked in a mirror and exclaimed, "Oh, my God! I'm a BABY!" It was as if her eternal self was peering out from the new body, surprised to discover that her timeless spirit was now encased in a chronologically younger body.

Another example of "out of the mouths of babes" solved a family mystery. Carol is a client and friend whose mother had suffered greatly from alcoholism. Her mother was thought to have committed suicide. It was suspected that she had taken barbiturates before jumping into a lake. Carol never believed this to be true.

A few years after her mother's passing, Carol's first grandson was born to her daughter. When her grandson was less than four years old, she was driving her daughter and the little boy around town on errands. Carol was talking and reminiscing about her own mother, while her daughter sat, listening attentively, in the front passenger seat. Suddenly Carol's grandson, who sat in the backseat, interrupted their conversation.

"Grandma, are you talking about your mommy?" he asked.

"Yes," Carol replied.

"She didn't kill herself!" he exclaimed.

"What do you mean?" Carol asked, astounded.

"She got tangled in the weeds!" her grandson said, with emphasis.

"How do you know that?" Carol could not believe what she was hearing.

"Because she told me, before I was born."

Then Carol's grandson calmly turned his attention back to the children's book that lay in his lap.

The new generation will be one of more and more souls returning, awakened. These are children entering with soul memories that prompt them to speak of events and objects that they could not have known, and who carry wisdom and visions that extend beyond the influences of their parents.

*The next stories demonstrate the positive effects of souls returning to the same families.*

## THE CIRCLE OF LIFE—AND LOVE

My daughter, Lori, was in constant prayer for her only child—my granddaughter—Brooke. Now twenty-one, Brooke had been drug addicted since she was sixteen years old—most recently injecting methamphetamines. We had no idea if she was dead or alive, since we had not heard from her in over three months. One night in desperation, Lori beseeched her own deceased grandmother (who had known and loved Brooke as a child). Lori prayed, "Muzzie, you are really there and you can hear me. Brooke needs your help. If you possibly can, go stop her!!! Please!!!"

A few months later, Brooke called me to say she was pregnant. I had learned of Brooke's pregnancy not long before my first reading with Louise in 1997. Louise was accurately describing some current groups and situations within which I was involved. Suddenly she said, "Pies . . . I see pies everywhere. Did your mother bake pies?" I acknowledged that pies were one of Mom's trademarks when she was alive. Louise then said, "Well, your mother is here and she wants you to know she's coming back as your grandchild or great-grandchild. She made her transition about eight years ago, didn't she?"

I was stunned, to say the least. I thought Louise might tell me of successes or turns in my career. My mother (who had passed on eight years before) was, right then, the furthest thing from my mind. Also, since I had just met Louise for the first time, I had not told her that I had children, let alone grandchildren!

Prior to my reading with Louise, upon discovering she was pregnant, Brooke had chosen to go into a drug rehab program for pregnant women and new mothers. The baby's father, Dave, also wanted to turn his life around. He sincerely wanted to be a husband and father. So he made a commitment to attend the drug treatment program for new fathers, even though it meant separation from Brooke until a month after the baby was born. This turn of events was stunning, to say the least. They were both working very hard to recover from their addictions and to take responsibility for this child.

Lori would later say to me, "When I asked Muzzie to stop Brooke, I never dreamed this is how she would do it!"

Louise, in her own inimitable way, was determined that my mother was coming back as Brooke's baby. She asked if Brooke knew Muzzie. I said, "Yes, they were very close. When she was a baby, she used to sit on Muzzie's lap." Louise replied, "Your mother says she will accomplish a lot on Brooke's lap."

With Brooke's history of drug abuse, I expressed my concern for the baby's health. Louise allayed my fears by saying, "This soul will come in with such momentum that it will blow out any residue of drugs, or else there is no residue." Then she said, "I've just asked your mother if there are any problems and she said, 'Only getting there!'" (Seemingly because so many souls were waiting to come in.) That remark certainly sounded like my mother!

Next, Louise suddenly said, "Your mother says to tell you she was there with you when you tried on her necklace last week." A week prior to my reading, while in the privacy of my own bedroom, I was dressing for a party. Though I hadn't touched it in eight years, I opened a box of Mom's jewelry and tried on a crystal necklace, then I put it back in the box. No one could have known this. Apparently Mom added this validation to confirm that all Louise was saying was really about to happen.

A few days after Mom passed away eight years before, my daughter, Lori, and I were reminiscing about her. Suddenly Lori saw a brilliant, iridescent green ball of light dancing between us. I couldn't see it myself, but Lori described it. We both believed it to be Muzzie's "soul energy."

On the morning after my reading, while looking out the window and dressing for work, I played the tape of my session with Louise. My windows face a large lagoon. The water still appeared rather dark since the sun was not up yet. When the tape reached the part about Muzzie coming back, suddenly there was a brilliant, iridescent green ball of light dancing back and forth across the water. In disbelief, I went out to see what was reflecting into the water, but there was nothing: no lights, no morning sun, nothing to reflect.

Then I remembered Lori's description eight years earlier of the green ball of light right after Muzzie passed on. I watched this light reappear and dance on the water for three days before sunrise. It was also seen by my neighbor. After three days it disappeared and has not been seen again.

All of this was just the beginning. Unaware of Louise's information, Brooke called her mother one day and said, "Mom, I feel so surrounded with love. I keep feeling that this baby is someone I already know!" With that remark, Lori and I shared the news that she would most likely give birth to her own great-grandmother.

"Oh, my God!" Brooke exclaimed, and then burst into peals of uncontrollable laughter at the thought of it. She had adored Muzzie. This news definitely fortified her commitment to a drug-free life. What a responsibility!

Sophie Lynn was born on July 31, 1997, healthy, bright and precocious, without a trace of any drug effects. Her parents maintain their commitment to live a drug-free life. They are embracing a very traditional, conservative lifestyle.

In the reading, Louise had said, "Your mother says she will let you know that it's her in several ways: When you put a ribbon in her hair, you'll know. (Muzzie knows that I've always known about a story concerning a special ribbon in her hair when she was five in 1907.) Also she will see something silver that used to belong to her, and she will run up to it and say, "That's mine, I want it!" She added that, when a toddler, she would look at a picture of Muzzie and ask curiously, "Who's that? Who's that?"

She is not yet old enough to say and do the things Louise said would signal to us her past identity; however, Sophie has exhibited many of the same traits that were characteristic of my mother. She is a mischievous, playful, vivacious go-getter. She eagerly walked at eight months and ran at nine months. They share a favorite food (bananas) and a favorite color (purple), the color Louise had mentioned in the reading. These could be called coincidences, but there have been too many other interesting validations.

When the baby was one month old, two relatives recalled that twenty years prior, my mother, who had never liked her given name, Agnes, said that she had always wished her name was Sophie.

My mother loved roses and had always taken great pride in her beautiful rose garden at her home in Kirbyville. This baby lives with her parents on Kirby Way in Roseville. Interesting? Just coincidence? Perhaps the soul chooses more of the conditions and circumstances of its life than we can possibly imagine.

When Sophie was eight months old, my daughter and I took her to have her portrait taken. The photographer wound up a music box and handed it to the baby. It played a very old song, rarely heard these days, a song called "Playmate" that had been my mom's favorite. It went something like, "Oh, little playmate, come out and play with me . . ." She used to sing it to my children and grandchildren. We had not heard it in years. Sophie, of course, was fascinated with the music box. We were frustrated because we knew the song, but couldn't remember the words.

Reentry: Choosing New Parents

Later, at home, we were talking while the baby sat on the floor, playing with her back to us. Suddenly the words to the song came to us and we began to sing. Sophie whirled her head around so fast she almost lost her balance. She looked intensely at me, then at Lori. A faraway look came into her eyes and she continued to stare while we sang the rest of the song. We were certainly as surprised as she was.

Years ago when the grandchildren would stay over at Mom's place, she would often engage them in a game of "Wahoo," her favorite board game. Everyone in the family has fond memories of taking turns yelling "Wahoo!" with each victory. When Sophie was seventeen months old, she was visiting with me at my home. Her crib was in my bedroom. We both were sound asleep when—in the middle of the night, piercing the silence—she yelled, "Wahoo!" Startled, I sat up and looked at her. She continued her sound sleep, her breathing relaxed and rhythmic. Needless to say, I remained awake for a while.

What a wonderful circle of life this is! This fascinating little person—my mother! Sophie is now almost two years old. Her mother, my granddaughter, Brooke, has just been told that in a few months she will give birth to triplets! Oh, my! I wonder who we will be welcoming back!

*Leslie Oliver*


## GOODNIGHT MOON

Howard and I met during my very first trip to London, in the late '80s. We had an idyllic, very romantic time together. It felt like a dream come true. He graciously treated me to short jaunts out of the city to historical places and quaint old inns. When I returned home from my visit, he wrote the kind of letters one keeps forever, tied up with a ribbon. He sent photos of where we'd walked through a glorious park, accented with one particular day, when I lamented that I'd left my camera behind. Later we rendezvoused once or twice in London and northern California—my home at the time—and our relationship quite naturally evolved into an enduring friends-across-the-sea sort of friendship.

So it was with no discomfort whatsoever that I eventually met Howard's new wife, Helga. They had met on holiday in Thailand. She relocated from her homeland in Germany and was adjusting to life in a new country.

I first saw Helga when she came to meet me at Heathrow Airport. I planned to stay the weekend with the two of them at their home in east London, before going on to London for speaking engagements and client consultations. Not many women would be prepared to drive to the airport at 5:00 in the morning to pick up their husband's former girlfriend.

She stood in the waiting area, where people watched for customs-cleared passengers, holding a copy of my book *Beyond Boundaries*, hoping to match the promo photo on the back with my travel-worn face. I thought that Howard was a lucky man to have married such an attractive and helpful lady.

The routine that she and Howard graciously provided has now evolved into a wonderful, nearly ten-year-old tradition for me. It allows me to fully recover from jet lag. They put me to bed with a Perrier on the nightstand, let me wake at my leisure and then take a welcome walk in nature and a meal in a pub or in their beautiful garden. They now live in Winchester, a perfect walk from their new home into town.

During my first visit with Helga, she expressed an interest in my work. Howard still saw it as pretty "booga-booga" stuff.

That first afternoon, as I chatted with her in the "lounge" (English living room), I was distracted by the image that I interpreted as her grandmother. She appeared to my upper right—over Helga's head—where I view souls who are awaiting reentry, rather than where I normally view souls on the Other Side.

"Excuse me, Helga," I began, "but I have to interrupt here for a moment. Your grandmother is here, wanting to communicate."

I love telepathy. It is so convenient. It's never any problem to translate limiting, linear language. Sometimes I'll view particular gestures that are built in to certain languages and cultures, but thought communication is not limited by language. It did not matter that Helga's grandmother had only spoken German.

Helga looked very receptive, so I continued. Our talk became a "mini-reading." I never bring through this information unsolicited, and rarely outside of consultations. But at this moment, it felt important for me to interpret for Helga's grandmother.

"She is showing me a white rose, a memory about ringing a little bell, and a message that has to do with some digging going on in a basement." Helga confirmed the personal significance of the white flower, the Christmas rose being her grandmother's favorite. She loved receiving it on her birthday, December 22. The ringing of the bell is done, as part of a very old tradition, the moment after "Christkind," the Christ child, has left the house. The candles are lit on the Christmas tree and the children are allowed into the room for the great moment of unwrapping their presents.

After my visit, Helga's father confirmed that her grandmother did bury her jewelry in the basement under the stairs of their house. The home had never been sold, but was taken away from the family when they had to flee after Germany lost the war. Her uncle visited his former home two years ago, but fearful owners didn't allow him to look around.

"Well," I continued, "here's what your grandmother really wants you to know. It seems that she will be returning as your firstborn child! She's not showing me the sex of the body she will 'inhabit'; it doesn't seem to matter. She or he will want to know all the names of the flowers in the garden, and will want your influence in guiding him or her spiritually. The heart-connection that you shared—and still share—is the corner-stone from which many good things will evolve when you are together again as mother and child."

Not too long after that visit, Tristen, a beautiful son, was born to Helga and Howard. When I received the announce-ment, I sent the children's book *Goodnight Moon* by Margaret Wise Brown. I thought it to be the perfect baby gift. The book has become a classic. Grandma Bunny sits with Baby Bunny in the great green room, where there is a comb and a brush and a picture of the cow jumping over the moon. On each page, the child looks to find where the teeny mouse is hiding. The room gets progressively darker, as the moon outside gets brighter, lulling the bunny to sleep.

By the time of my next visit with my friends, Tristen was a toddler with a baby brother named Richard. Tristen is a very sensitive, physically beautiful, almost delicate-looking little boy. Little Richard is a tank. He is all boy, with a wonderful, quick sense of humor that he uses to help his older brother lighten up and take himself less seriously.

The evening of my arrival, Helga thanked me for sending the book. She said, "I didn't tell you this that day that you tuned in to my grandmother, but my grandmother had been raped by the Russians during the war. She forgave them, because she knew how the Nazis were treating the Russians. She always became so thoughtful about the past when we'd look together at the moon at night!"

Tristen then entered the room where we were talking. He took me by the hand and escorted me up to his bedroom. He took the book I had sent, placed it on his little table and very deliberately turned each page, pointing to the moon—getting brighter and brighter—on each page. He completely ignored the little mouse. Then Tristen again took me by the hand and pulled me over to his window. He pointed up to the moon, as if to say, "Sheee's baaack!"

The next day Howard and Helga took Tristen out on errands, while I baby-sat for Richard. When they returned, Helga said that on the drive home, Tristen continually asked, "Will my friend Lu-eeze be thea when we get heome, my friend, Lu-eeze?" This isn't the first time that I have met a child for whom I've interpreted before they were born. They do seem to recognize or remember, on some level of consciousness, that we met when they were still in spirit!

I went on into London after that visit, and called back to Helga to thank her for the weekend. Tristen answered the phone, then I heard him announce loudly, "Mummy! It's Lu-eeze!" Helga came to the phone, amazed at Tristen, who had never answered the phone, nor ever announced anyone like that.

It's fun to observe Tristen as he grows, knowing that he embodies both female and male aspects as we all do, but watching the threads that Tristen's soul carries—from Helga's grandmother into Tristen—is fascinating.

Helga's grandmother loved her garden. I've watched Tristen—from the time he could first walk—follow his daddy around in the garden with his pint-size watering can, mimicking every one of Howard's gardening gestures. Helga's grandmother loved to cook. I chuckle when I watch Tristen stand on his stool beside his "mum," cooking together with her. He has his grandmother's bright blue eyes and loves herbal tea. His little brother dislikes it immensely. Helga later reminded me that her grandmother had shown me her favorite teapot in her reading.

Helga's grandmother was very fashionable. Helga said that she "had a feeling for dressing very smart at all times. She was a real lady." During one of my visits, I came down the stairs with a scarf tied around my neck. Tristen looked up at me and declared, "I d'nt lyke thet scof thet yewr weearing. I'd pit sumtheeng else wif it!"

Helga feels that her grandmother's love for travel—an unusual one for most people her age in Germany—must have been an incentive for her to return to parents who travel extensively. First, it may provide the opportunity for her to learn to trust that the world can be a safe place. Second, she may expand from the challenge of living in a new and different society, alongside her granddaughter, all the while supporting Helga as she grows from doing the same.

Indeed, Tristen is here to be Tristen. The spirit of Helga's grandmother chose Helga and Howard for parents who would help advance its soul's growth. When I pick up certain "threads," which the soul carries from previous life experiences, I can communicate for that soul what it wants to carry into this life—to expand its learning or to resolve old issues—and what it can now leave behind. Regression therapists can quite effectively help clients reach—and thereby heal—inhibiting fears and patterns that do not relate to the client's present life. I enjoy finding the threads that confirm to clients that they are eternal, evolving souls, choosing the parents that will support their growth.

## GRANDFATHER MEETS HIMSELF

*In recent years I've encountered more and more souls who are "re-cycling" or reincarnating back into the same families, and "sooner" (that is, with fewer generations between incarnations) in earth years, for there is no time on the Other Side. Since many souls are now, ideally, returning to the physical dimension in a more awakened state, they can do more good by rejoining with previous family members from a new and different perspective. I've also found this reuniting effect occasionally with friends who come together again into the same family. For example, I discovered that a client's buddy and airplane copilot, who had been killed in Vietnam, had returned as my client's son. They are currently working out many issues through the son's critical illnesses. Whatever configuration will stimulate and support a soul's growth—balance old issues and bring about opportunities to open hearts—makes this possible and advantageous. Whatever works. The next story is an example of this trend.*

Susan arrived with her four-month-old baby in her arms. She asked if I would mind if she nursed him during the consultation. I said that I wouldn't mind. I couldn't wait for my usual invocation to tell her what I was seeing: "This baby is your grandfather-come-back!"

"I thought so," she said, smiling.

I began then, in my customary manner, and was taking inventory of all the information—past-present-probable future and looking for any souls coming forward from the Other Side—when an image of Susan's grandfather appeared directly in back of her, standing behind the couch. I explained to her how it is possible that an aspect of her grandfather's spirit can be reexperiencing life in the physical form of her young son, while still presenting itself as if on the Other Side, as her grandfather. It's confusing for us to understand this, because in this dimension we relate so much to one's physicality and locality. Our expansive, eternal energy, not existing exclusively in the physical, can be several places at once.

"Your grandfather is smiling down on you. He's showing me a fond memory of a long car ride with you through a long stretch of desert. He remembers a special conversation that you shared."

"I know the trip and the conversation he's referring to! It was memorable," she reflected.

"Now he's pointing to the baby and wants you to know of all that he hopes to accomplish in that body," I continued. Just then, Susan's grandmother appeared beside her grandfather. The baby pulled his head away from where he was nursing at his mother's breast, looked up at the grandmother and laughed!

"Of course!" I exclaimed. "This grandmother has been his wife!" This was starting to feel like a three-ring circus, and I was announcing all the acts. "What's next?" I wondered. When we concluded the session, Susan bundled up the baby and set him in his infant seat carrier that sat on the floor by her feet. I leaned down to coo with the baby.

Suddenly I caught his thoughts, telepathically. "He can't wait to have a bicycle!" I relayed to Susan.

"That's funny," she said. "My mother was just visiting for a few weeks. I told her that I'm looking forward to the children getting older, so we can all get bicycles. My mother said, "Why get bicycles, when you can walk!"

"I guess that he heard every word!" I said, amazed at consciousness that is aware of all that is, no matter the chronological age of the body. I had experienced this with clients' relatives who suffer from Alzheimer's or lie in comas, and even with clients' pets. But this was the first time I'd experienced telepathy with an infant.

On her way out, Susan expressed the great contentment she felt from receiving confirmation that the loving bundle in her arms did indeed carry forward the heart-link that had developed with her beloved grandfather when she was the child.

## Becoming a Receiver: Trust Telepathy

I always stop to confirm to someone when they have just been telepathic with me. Don't hesitate to do the same for others. The only difference between telepathy with others in this physical dimension and with souls on the Other Side is that it's more difficult to check back with that soul to get confirmation about the message they have sent you, what you sense they communicated telepathically. In those cases, synchronicities will often guide you, as they have for clients in many of these stories.

People are telepathic all the time but just don't realize it. Recently a man sat down next to me at a restaurant counter. Suddenly he started whistling the song "Every little breeze seems to whisper Louise. . . ." That same week, I overheard two women having dinner next to me at a Chinese restaurant, scheming to come up with a credible lie to tell a friend whom they'd forgotten to include. "Just tell her the truth," I thought to myself.

"Maybe we should just tell her the truth," one of the women said, immediately after my thoughts.

A few years ago, I was taking a break from seeing clients in Chicago. I decided to walk down the street to a hair salon to get my bangs trimmed. The receptionist asked me to wait for the operator, far to my left, where he was finishing up with a customer.

I looked at the operator next to him. He was slouched down in his chair, reading a newspaper. There were little piles of hair cuttings on the floor, all around his chair. "Why doesn't he sweep up the hair?" I thought to myself. Then I asked myself, "Why does it matter to me?" The young man stood up, laid his newspaper in the chair and started to walk toward me.

One of the side effects of being able to see beyond time and space is that when I encounter someone I have known in another life space, I often "see double." I might describe the sensation as seeing a double exposure or an overlay of one time period on another. I experience the individual in the present time, while relating to the person in that other time simultaneously. This can become a bit distracting, as it was in this instance.

I suddenly saw an overlay of this young haircutter as a neighbor in northern Europe a couple of hundred years ago, in a very agrarian lifetime where we all depended on working the land for our survival. We were both male. He was complaining about not having any money. "Why don't you work your land, man?" I was saying to him in that other life space. In present time, here, I was thinking, "Why doesn't he sweep up the hair?"

The fellow looked directly at me. I said to him, "Have you ever been to the restaurant down the block? They make the best homemade soup." Then my thoughts went to thinking about the fragrant cinnamon rolls I'd noticed there. Just like my mother used to make, I thought to myself.

"Yeah," the man replied, "and don't they make cinnamon rolls just like your mother used to make?"

"You were just being telepathic," I said to him.

"Uh huh," he said, "I do that sometimes."

CHAPTER FOUR

# The Future Can Change the Present

*D*oes time play tricks on you? Sometimes it feels like there isn't enough of it. Other times, it feels like it's not passing fast enough. Does time speed up when you're awake in the middle of the night? Does it disappear when you're having a good time?

It's true. Time is playing with you. It knows just when to sneak up on you, take you by surprise and when to run away. You are involved in an intimate relationship with time. It can dominate, frustrate, tease, dare, humiliate and control you. Time can run your life. It can ruin your life. But there's hope. It doesn't have to.

Your relationship with time depends on how you perceive it. The way you relate to time influences how it interacts with you. Like so many things in life, it gets easier to handle when you change your understanding of it. Perhaps the following ideas will help.

Time is an illusion. Time only exists in this reality because we experience it as linear and sequential. Events seem to occur one at a time, and one after the other. If you can step out of your current reality—as I do in consultations—you would experience all time (or no time) as coexisting.

Princeton physicist John Wheeler coined the term "black hole" to refer to collapsing stars that crunch not only matter but also the space around it, bringing time there to an end. "Time cannot be an ultimate category in the description of nature," he declares. " 'Before' and 'after' don't rule everywhere."

I experience this phenomenon when I meet with clients. I'm able to go beyond time and view the past, present and probable future where all time is still—and already—occurring. Over the phone, I can "tune in" to clients anywhere in the world. I simply access a frequency that connects us and retrieve information from where their energy exists beyond time and the limitations of physical proximity.

In 1905 Albert Einstein presented his special theory of relativity, which holds that the measurement of time intervals is affected by the motion of the observer. Two years later a mathematician, Hermann Minkowski, proposed a new geometry that adds time to the three dimensions of space (height, width, and depth). This four-coordinate system—space-time—caught on as an efficient way to simplify Einstein's formulas.

An example of the idea of relativity is when you're seated in a train and notice that the train next to yours begins to move. It's quite disorienting. Is it moving or are you? You don't know until you see a third reference point, like the platform. That's relative motion.

In a similar way, time is relative. But there is no ultimate platform. We don't notice the differences because they are infinitesimally small. Time seems nonexistent when you're awake in the middle of the night because you lack a reference to where you are in it. There's no backdrop—people coming and going, variations in the sunlight outside—against which to gauge it.

I often refer to John Boslough's recollection of graffiti that he observed on a cafe wall in Texas: "Time is nature's way of keeping everything from happening all at once." In his article "The Enigma of Time" (*National Geographic,* March 1990), he reminds us that children before the age of two have little sense of the passage of time and that it may have been the same for our early ancestors. Some scholars believe that people once lived in a state of "timeless present" with little or no sense of past or future.

He mentions an old Hopi Indian woman in northern Arizona, who talks of a close friend, dead for several years, as if he just stepped out the door. Hopi verbs make no distinction between past and present. All time runs together, something like an ever-continuing present. Clocks and calendars support the illusion that we live in a world of mathematically measured segments of time. But physical time is relative. It depends on things that happen—how we perceive them to be happening—in our outer world. Time is not happening to us.

It's one thing for me to do what I do and quite another for me to understand how I do it. For this reason I began to explore the concept of time. I needed to understand how it is that I am able to move into expanded consciousness and view clients' past childhoods, their past lives and their potential, positive future moments. I also needed to understand how I am able to access both the consciousness of souls preparing to reenter and the consciousness of souls simply presenting themselves from the Other Side, apparently existing and perceiving beyond time. Once I "tune in" to any of these "frequencies," I can move events forward and backward in time.

I started to understand that sequential, linear time, as we know it in this physical, third-dimensional reality is, like death, an illusion. Where Einstein's theory of relativity explains that "time is relative to where the observer is standing," I realized that I must be going to a frequency within myself that takes me to expanded consciousness, outside of this linear time framework.

When I experience "no time"—past, present and most probable, positive future—all exist in the now. I've trained myself to receive information only under these conditions. I do occasionally, however, get "bleedthroughs"—that is, when I encounter someone with whom, or find myself in a location where, I have a past-life (another time/space) connection. Then it feels as though I'm straddling two time periods simultaneously. (Sometimes people suspect or they fear or they hope that I'm "tuning in" all the time. I ask them, "Why would I *want* to do that?")

The future does not come after the past and present, and the past does not come before the present and future. It's all the same to me, the way these scenes appear. First, I relax myself and invite the client to join me in taking a deep breath. This gets us "in sync" with each other. Then I recite my invocation.

Then I take inventory of the scenes that start to appear to me. Next, I funnel the information down into a linear timeline: I place information about the present directly in front of me. The past—childhood and past lives—go to my left. Up to my right, I see souls who are preparing to reenter. Farther to my right is where I sort out the future scenes. Farthest in that direction is where I view souls—all of whom have gone to the Light—who come forward from the non-physical dimension, from the "Other Side."

Even though I know that linear time is an illusion—and that it is all occurring at the same time—no concept is useful unless it proves to be relevant to my clients' lives.

The next two stories document the first two consultations where playing with the illusion of time became quite functional in other ways.

## BEN

*I was in the middle of a session with Cathy when I moved into a moment in her future consciousness, for the purpose of creating a pathway from her present to her highest potential future. This helps a client face forward—now, in the present. Repositioning clients in this way also creates a stronger pull from "here" to "there."*

*I said to her, "In this future moment, there is a 'Ben' on the Other Side, who wants to thank Michael for holding his hand."*

*Cathy replied, "Ben is my husband Michael's stepfather. But Ben is still in the hospital. He hasn't died yet!"*

I remember Cathy, my wife, telling me about the message Louise relayed from Ben in a future moment, from the Other Side. It definitely influenced my actions. During the time from November 1996 until his death on January 1, 1997, I was reading voraciously and quickly incorporating my reading into a transformation of consciousness. These things were all background, leading up to the activities around Ben's death. Important books at that time were Deepak Chopra's *The Path to Love*, and Neale Donald Walsch's *Conversations with God*,

*Book 1*. In that context, I heard a one-line message from Cathy (really from Ben through Louise) about my holding Ben's hand.

Ben had a stroke the second week of December in Valley Forge, Pennsylvania. I drove from Baltimore every few days to visit. He was in the ICU and had a steady downhill course in the hospital, including the insertion of a breathing tube for about ten days. When the tube was removed he had little ability to speak, but he had periods of awareness.

As the end approached, one night I took my teenage daughters to say good-bye. My twin sister, who lives in L.A., was also there. Ben was pretty alert, recognized the girls, and was non-verbally responsive. He was more alert than he had been for days. I think he was more alert because I was speaking to him as if he were fully conscious.

My mother and their friends tended to avoid real conversation with him, maybe because they were so scared and bottled up themselves. I think that his true situation had not really been explained to him, and he was experiencing a lot of fear and confusion. I simply explained to him that he had had a stroke, leaving him with impaired vision. I said that this must be confusing to him, and that he should not be afraid.

As the end of visiting hours approached, I received a message (in my head) to stay with him. Staying wouldn't have been a terribly unusual thing for me to do since I am a pediatrician and have spent hours and days and nights in hospitals caring for desperately ill patients. This was different, as I had never helped someone transition to the Other Side. To get a message to stay was out of the ordinary in this case, as Ben and I had never truly had a personal conversation in the fifteen years that we lived in the same house—between the time I was six and twenty-one years of age—nor, for that matter, during the nearly forty-five years he had been my stepfather.

I received permission from the nurses to stay and went to his bedside. I told him in simple details about his clinical condition. I told him that the end was probably near, and that he should have no fear. With what I had learned from Raymond Moody's work, I described for him the concept of being out of body and the tunnel with the light at the end. I then told him that all his relatives would be waiting for him and that he would be shocked at what a wonderful "life" he had in store for him. Then I told him to look for Louise and use her to communicate directly with me. He listened.

I was sitting at his bedside. He was on his back, propped with pillows, breathing rapidly. I offered him ice chips and frequently bathed his mouth with a sponge on a stick, imbedded with some hospital potion. He was appreciative and alternated between sleeping and semiwakefulness. I was sitting right next to his bed reading, when he struggled to cough, which woke him up. I gave him ice chips and for the first time in my life, I started to talk to him about our lives together.

We reminisced about his parents, my childhood activities, ball games we went to, his friends and relatives. During the conversation I reached up and took his hand in mine. It was soft and frail and cool. I could feel the love coming through it. It was the first time I ever held his hand, except to cross the street as a young child. It felt wonderful. For the next hours I spoke, he listened and nodded in response. I stroked his arm and held his hand. Love was expressed between us for the first time as a conscious two-way communication.

In these hours Ben gave to me one of the most profound spiritual experiences of my life. I was in a state of bliss throughout the night. In the morning he felt better, and I left the hospital with the sun coming in the room, the nurses giving Ben a sponge bath and joking playfully with him. Back at my mother's apartment I gathered together my mom, my sister, the children, the nieces and the nephews.

I described the night and told them that I knew that he was on his way to heaven. I told them that it was important for them to speak the truth clearly to him now, that he was not afraid, and that he could help them with their fears and difficulty in communicating with him. The next day he died peacefully in his sleep.

About a month later, I saw Louise and she had a message for me from Ben that he had made it easily to the Other Side, that everything was fine, and he thanked me for holding his hand and helping me. He offered me his love.

*Michael Rakoff*

## MOON OVER THE LAKE

A couple of years after my mother passed over, I had the opportunity to sit down with Louise for the first time. My mother had led a difficult life here on earth. I felt a need to know that she was okay. To my surprise, the first people to pop in to talk with me were my grandparents, who had been very special to me. My grandma, a very conservative German, wanted me to know that she applauded me for the moments in my life when I've said, "I'll be damned if I'm going to let society dictate to me what is acceptable and what is not!" That unexpected message from my grandma has given me strength over time as I continue to live an "unconventional" life.

My mother came forth and shared bits and pieces of information that reassured me that it was she with whom we were communicating. Then, well into this conversation, Louise asked if it is possible to see water from my bed. I said, "Yes!" Then she asked, "Can you see the moon from your bed?" I said, "Yes!" She paused, trying to interpret. "There is something about the moon over the water at night, and you knowing your mother is there."

Louise then listed a few types of flowers, my mother's passion. We settled on geraniums. Mom liked geraniums and planted them everywhere. Louise's comment made me laugh, because the geranium had never been my favorite flower. Louise added that there was something about a future moment where there would be something about that flower and a moment of realization when I would know that my mother would be there with me.

In the following months, I kept the information—about the moon, the water and the geranium—in the back of my mind. I live in the hills of an oceanside community with a lovely view of the Pacific Ocean. I thought about the message sometimes in the early hours, when I would watch the full moon cast a beautiful reflection on the waves, but I never felt my mother in those moments. I had placed a pot of geraniums at the entrance of my home. I would think of my mother on occasion when looking at them, but never felt my mother there with me. After a year or more, I stopped looking for the signals to which Louise had alerted me.

Two years passed, and then my family had an unexpected opportunity to spend a week at a very special summer home in northern Wisconsin's great North Woods. My dad's father had built the home. It had been in our family for four generations. This summer home had been my mother's bliss. Whenever Dad would talk about selling the place, Mom would exclaim, "You'll have to sell it over my dead body." After she died, he did just that. He sold the summer home, along with everything in it.

This special opportunity that summer brought my sisters, their families, my dad and me to an unforgettable moment, sitting on the deck of this summer home, overlooking a magnificent view of the lake. It was more beautiful than I'd remembered. I thought to myself, this must be heaven! I never dreamed that I would ever see this view again, especially with my family surrounding me. I had no doubt that Mother had played a part in making this happen.

I didn't want to remember that the house now belonged to someone else. It had been such a part of my family's history. It seemed very odd to me that the new owners had not changed or moved one thing—not a dish, not a curtain, not one piece of art. Even my childhood stereo was in its place. Everywhere I looked, I was reminded of my mother's flare for decorating and I thought of her. She was there!

The first night I bunked in the same room with my niece. She is addicted to those wonderful wave machines, and cannot sleep without them. She selected the setting "waterfall," which sounded to me like scraping concrete. In the middle of the night, I took my blanket with me to sleep in the living room. I curled up on the sofa, exhausted.

I raised my head to adjust my position and there in front of my eyes was the most amazing view I have ever seen. A huge, deep orange harvest moon hung low over the water, perfectly positioned in the center of the lake. I was mesmerized by the moon's beam of light illuminating this magnificent scene in its entirety. I knew at that moment that Mom was there with me. I asked her to help me get some sleep, and sleep I did soundly.

The exterior of the summer home had flower boxes below almost every window, along with many scattered plant containers on decks and walkways of the property. Every single flower box and container had been planted with red geraniums! Mom's favorite flower in her favorite color. The new owners had planted red geraniums everywhere! In my last moment before departing, my sister took a picture of me sitting next to a bowl of red geraniums, a beautiful view of the lake in the background. In that moment, I knew that Mom felt our tears.

I had my second visit with Louise two years later. It was equally informative. My mother popped in first thing to say, "Hello!" Mom went on to confirm that she had just been with Dad and me "where there are the colors pink and gray." Dad had, in fact, recently visited me at my home, which is decorated predominantly in pinks and grays! Mom went on to express her concern about Dad's thoughts and fears, his feeling of emptiness about his own death.

My father is agnostic and does not believe in an afterlife. Mom urged me to start preparing him for an afterlife. Knowing Dad, she acknowledged the difficulty of such a task. She guaranteed me that just a few words would face him in the right direction to make his transition easier.

The conversation continued. Then Louise said—much to her own surprise—that now my father was talking to me from the Other Side in the future! Please remember that as I write this, my father is still very much alive and in his body. It felt very odd to be receiving this information.

It was obvious that it was my dad for whom Louise was interpreting specific information from a future moment! The specifics were personal and unmistakable, concerning signed documents and family business. I was marveling at the time sequence—or should I say, the lack of any time sequence! Louise often reminds me that time is not sequential like we think. This certainly was proof!

Louise was amused by my dad. Now he was the one urging me to open up his mind to a deeper, more spiritual perspective while he was still in his body! In the future—looking back at his life from the Other Side—he was quite frustrated by his lack of acceptance concerning so much that my mom and I had always trusted. Then Dad thanked me for the conversation "about driving." In the present, I had been worrying over how to tell Dad not to drive the eight hours it takes to visit me. He was conveying his gratitude for a conversation that I hadn't yet figured out how to communicate! So now I know what I have to do. This will be no small feat to accomplish.

Dad is a pilot. In the future moment—from the Other Side—he was excited about communication in his afterlife, describing it as "very radarlike." He reassured me that he would be in touch in the future. He told Louise that in one instance, I will be driving and will know—unmistakably—that he is there. Dad and I share a love of driving. For now, I will enjoy my father while he is here. I will not look too hard for the "signs" that Louise indicated. They will be revealed in their right timing. I also know that Mom and Dad will always be with me.

*Debra*

## BEST FRIEND AND FUTURE SON

*The revelation that occurred in this consultation left even me a bit incredulous. It came in from the future and was confirmed in the present. It was an amazing demonstration of the timeless nature of our souls and the powerful nature of the heart-link that allows us to maintain relationships with friends—beyond time— when it can further our soul's growth.*

Judy works a day job with a small record company and plays in a "chick band" whenever her group gets gigs in and around Manhattan. It came to the point in her consultation where I usually sort of hang out in a future moment in order to determine what's new and different for my clients by that time—how they have potentially grown spiritually. I found (experienced) her looking out onto an expansive green lawn in one of those future moments.

It appeared to be at the front of a large home rather than on a golf course. It could have been a location where her band was playing; it could have been her own future home. She seemed to be awaiting someone's arrival. She stood on the top step at the front of the structure, focusing on a car that was slowly making its way up a long driveway.

Just then, a little boy appeared at the bottom step, smiling up at Judy. It felt like she was now watching her own son. He toddled slowly up one step at a time, climbing toward her. As she watched him, I collected her thoughts and interpreted to her, "When you think about this little boy, you're knowing that he has a direct connection to someone on the Other Side." This made no sense at this point, and I proceeded in another direction, describing memories that she held in that future moment—about her past—that would enlighten her about changing patterns in her present.

Then I was pulled back to another future moment. At that time, a soul on the Other Side—one whom Judy had known as a female—wanted to confirm something to her. It had to do with an agreement or a decision that had been made before her passing. There was a lot of information for me to sort out here. It seemed that this soul was coming forward for the most usual purpose, to confirm that she was still in touch with her friend. At the same time, she was presenting herself as a soul who had picked a prospective parent. She had chosen Judy!

Then I moved on to information that I was receiving about some circumstances that were involving her in the present. I mentioned the name Vicky, interpreting that she was one who was very much in need of her services at that time. Judy confirmed that she was assisting with a female friend who was critically ill.

Vicky was gay, and though Judy had recently eloped with her fiancé, she felt as though she had fallen in love with Vicky. Judy expressed her love for her friend, as well as her happiness in her new marriage. She was still confused by the intense feelings she had for Vicky.

She said that she and Vicky had actually discussed the possibility of them reuniting one day, possibly as mother and child. Vicky liked Judy's husband, a very warm and intelligent man. She once commented, "He'd make a great father."

So it seems that Vicky, critically ill in Judy's present, was communicating to her from the future, from the Other Side, about plans to reenter as her son. The future moment that I first described to Judy at the beginning of her session seemed to be the manifestation of the whole plan! The little boy she watched as he climbed the stairs was Vicky, her dear friend, returned.

## Becoming a Receiver: Create a Sacred Space

It is important for you to sculpt out a special nook in your home that is your private place. It might just be the corner of a room. Put a few of your special things in this space. You might want to create an altar. This is a place for you to pray, meditate, to write in a journal, to review and interpret your dreams, to be quiet with yourself, to come back to center. This is a place to reconnect with the Source, to surrender and ask for clear, gentle road signs, to feel what is unique and special about you.

B. F. Skinner, the father of behavior modification, was known to remain seated at his desk only while engaged in focused, intentional concentration. If his thoughts wandered, he would remove himself from that environment.

Behavioral principles define discriminative stimuli ("ds's") as environmental cues that become paired with specific behaviors. Over time, that stimuli will occasion that particular, paired behavior. For example, a sign that advertises a restaurant has been paired, in your repertoire of experience, with the behavior of eating. Whatever signals or advertises "restaurant" will occasion or stimulate thoughts of eating. When you sit quietly, meditatively, in your sacred space, that area will eventually support, and eventually occasion, serenity—a deeper, quieter place within yourself.

———————— **TRY THIS** ————————

Find your sacred space. Clear it out, clean it out, sculpt it to your liking. Add a few nice touches, something colorful, soft. Take a few moments to gather up a small assortment of precious things. You might find a picture of yourself as a child, a special object—a shell that you brought home from the beach or a rock from the mountains, something creative you've made, anything that holds special meaning for you. Put them on a little table, stool or shelf in your sacred space. This is your space. This is where you will honor yourself and come home to yourself.

# CHAPTER FIVE

# Continuing Missions

*I*t would appear in "consensus reality"—the general, workaday worldview we're often encouraged to assume—that life begins with birth and ends at death. If so, then one's soulful intentions, heartfelt passions, acquired knowledge and innate wisdom, spiritual enlightenment and God-given talents would end as well. The expanded view that my work and intuitive talents give me, as well as a very deep inner sense, confirms for me that these all stay with us when we leave behind our bodies. Quite often I find that an ongoing soul mission may direct us over many lifetimes, whether we're in or out of a physical body.

I come upon evidence of these soul missions in occasional consultations. It really does appear as though our soul's evolution is operating in a continuum of no-time, picking up from where it left off in one life's adventure, to expand, contribute and sometimes complete a mission in the next.

The following examples demonstrate the continuation of important missions—which are progressing quite nicely—by a few individual souls now on the Other Side.

The first report involves information that was received from a whole committee of souls on the Other Side! The second tells of emphatic instructions from a recently deceased husband and father to his wife and son, regarding the continuation of his work as an environmental biologist. There is my own experience of maintaining contact with Willis Harman, past president of the Institute of Noetic Sciences, a well-loved, internationally acclaimed visionary, who led business and spiritual leaders, scientists, philosophers and conscious seekers in the shift from a pragmatic, scientific worldview to a more holistic, unified and spiritual perspective. Finally, you'll read an example of the heart-link connecting me with a dear friend, before and after his passing.

## THE COMMITTEE OF COMEDIANS

I raced in a cab down the crisp, impatient Manhattan streets, glancing at my watch. It was an early autumn afternoon and I felt slightly anxious as I went to my first appointment with Louise. I knew I would be gone longer than I had anticipated from my frenetic investment banking office, on the excuse of having a doctor's appointment. Or should I have told my boss that I was off to see my intuitive spiritual counselor? At that time, I valued my job.

Louise imparted many thought-provoking insights during the session. However, two in particular dramatically altered the course of my life. She asked me if there was anyone in my life preparing to go to the "Other Side." Initially no one came to mind. She asked about an "S," and I immediately thought of my friend Sammy, who was an old-time burlesque comedian in his mid-eighties, whose health had begun to fail. I knew it was he, Sammy.

Louise told me she was going to a future moment where Sammy had already died and that his soul, from that vantage point, wanted to thank me for my assistance in helping him make the transition.

Louise spoke and said, "He thanks you for encouraging him to go to the Light."

I sat there a little disoriented, wondering what it was that I was meant to do.

"This has not been the first time you have been together," she continued. "You have helped each other many times. You have a true heart connection."

I asked her for a few specifics, feeling a little pressured that I had such a role mapped out for me in the future. She told me that I simply would know when I had to go to Sammy. Then she moved on to other subjects. Louise also mentioned that should I have an interest in developing my intuitive powers, I should consider an apprenticeship with her. This was a monumental suggestion, although I didn't recognize it at the time.

I had a very full life then and did not concentrate on what Louise told me. A number of months later, my husband and I were driving around on our first anniversary and, out of the blue, I suggested going to visit Sammy in his retirement home. This was something we had done together many times, and although the timing seemed inconvenient, my husband kindly complied. Usually he accompanied me, although it depressed him to see all of the older people struggling in the final stage of their lives. But this time he asked if he could stay outside and work on the engine of his van while I made my visit. It was late afternoon as I moved to Sammy's room, which was in the convalescent area.

Each time I had visited him previously, his roommate had been an ever-present, yet silent, fixture in the room. The late afternoon light shot through the trees, leaving patterns on the linoleum. Sammy was alone and in hospice care. He drifted in and out of dementia and pain. I took his hand in mine and told him how much he meant to so many people, how his performances on the stage and his comedy uplifted so many out of their misery, that his life had been worthwhile and that it was now time to go to the Light.

Sammy was a grandfather figure to me. Louise's words were not in my mind, at least not my conscious mind, as I soothed him, comforted him and directed him to the Light. Sammy would moan and go somewhere else and return with great clarity and focus in his eyes.

I am so thankful that we were alone for this parting. At one point, Sammy looked at me, into me, with such pure communication and love. I just clenched his hands and told him that I knew, at the moment, that he felt confused and that this feeling was temporary, that he had accomplished a great deal and should move toward the Light. He then looked at me and told me that he loved me. I have never felt such pure love and understanding as with this eighty-six-year-old gentleman on the cusp of death.

Two days later, Sammy died. My last moments with him were extraordinary, provoking such love, commitment and trust within my being. I knew that Louise had played a large part in this interaction. I had known what I was supposed to do, although it was not at all on the forefront of my mind and came quite naturally.

I joined forces with a mutual friend of Sammy's and mine to produce a tribute on Broadway to Sammy's comic genius and generous spirit six weeks later. We overcame numerous obstacles in our path and, as a young woman in my late-twenties, I committed myself as never before to an end that was beyond myself: not graduate school, nor self-advancement but a memorial to a long-forgotten, yet important part of America's comic heritage. We cut together two original short films, screened selections of Sammy's film work, and brought together a formidable grouping of comic greats to pay homage to him. The tribute was held in a historic theater on 42nd Street, where he made his name in the 1930s.

Although, to be honest, I was too sleep deprived and stressed to fully be in the moment, I cannot describe my feelings upon hearing the sound of laughter expanding within that theater for a comedian's work that had been, for the most part, shuffled aside and forgotten. I helped make that renaissance happen.

Louise had mentioned a heart connection between Sammy and me. Having always been an intellectual sort, this unanalyzable loyalty and love for this forgotten clown shifted the focus of my life.

After the tribute, I avidly pursued an apprenticeship with Louise and simultaneously worked to develop a nonprofit group in New York dedicated to preserving the traditions of classic comedians and translating their artistry into modern forms.

I have never felt so driven, and it was a perfect time to have this develop, just as I was being tempted to dive into the corporate opulence surrounding me. I danced the line, trying to accommodate both spheres in my life, but in the end, I had to honor my creative path and left my investment banking job.

Sammy dedicated his life to making people laugh, to uplifting them from their everyday miseries and making them feel part of a community, enjoying the foibles of human nature together. I knew that I needed more from life than the accumulation of money.

My apprenticeship with Louise encouraged me to trust my intuition and the timing of events and the synchronicity that informs all that we do. At times, the visions she shared with me were so fantastic and so specific that it was difficult not to want to follow them literally as truth. What I found was that when I tried to interpret her visions with my rational mind, I would be far off the map. Yet certain things would occur—often out of nowhere—that would confirm her predictions.

More than once, Louise helped me trust my communication with Sammy, who had been communicating with me in my dreams. One time he was actually showing me a rogues' gallery of comedians—unfamiliar to me—whom he identified with name titles below each face.

After the tribute, Louise and I began working, not only with Sammy, but also with a committee of well-known, classic comedians who had already passed on, who wanted to help me bring forward comedy that uplifts the human spirit rather than denigrates it. The fruits of these labors will be apparent in the future. I am grateful for the work I have done with Louise. My perspective is much broader and more expansive.

Continuing Missions                                                    **109**

When my mother recently died of a sudden illness, I felt the tremendous loss of a best friend, but not the tragedy of losing someone forever. I felt her presence and her love immediately and, at the time, I contacted Louise about writing this segment. I had no intention of asking about my mother, yet Louise gave me a couple of messages. One was to confirm the communication I felt between my mother and me, and to say that I would have a sign of this contact when I saw "pink over my right shoulder."

At the time, I was coordinating her memorial service to be held at sunset with pink and white balloons. I anticipated getting my "sign" at that time. Of course, that didn't happen. Yet the day after the service, the helpful neighbor who came out of the woodwork to direct the service stopped by our house to drop off a bud vase with little pink roses. She said that I might want to place that by my bedside as a reminder of my mother.

My life since her death had been packed with tasks and obligations. I was exhausted, too tired to do anything about the vase of roses. Later that night, I retired to my bed early and found myself awake and wanting to speak to my mother. I began to think in my mind, "Are you there? Are you listening?" and tried holding a conversation with my dead mother.

After about ten minutes, my husband opened the door and quietly placed the bud vase of pink roses on my night table. I had been lying on my left side and turned over my right shoulder to see what was going on. At that moment I understood Louise's prediction of "pink over my right shoulder" and felt rushes up and down my spine. My rational mind had predicted this "confirmation" happening in other situations but, as one will find with life and intuition, these blessings occur at truly unexpected and unpredictable times.

*Tracy*

## MESSAGES FROM WILLIS

I met Willis Harman about ten years before the end of his life. Greta, my niece, was serving as temporary director of the World Business Academy, a sister organization of the Institute of Noetic Sciences. Willis was the former president of IONS and a well-loved, world-famous visionary who "walked that walk" that bridged the two worlds of science (having taught engineering at Stanford) and the spiritual and esoteric.

Willis was a sort of grandfather figure to Greta. He consulted with and advised her, particularly when she was working for the WBA. When she gave Willis a copy of the introductory tape I use to prepare new clients, he expressed an interest in meeting me. For such a busy man, he had an amazing way of making unhurried time available for people he supported and cared about.

Each time I met with Willis, he would express his support for my work by asking—with enthusiasm—"So, how shall we collaborate?" We could never come up with a plan, but his never-ending gesture and faith in my work will never be forgotten.

A few months after his passing, I was walking down Sixth Avenue in Manhattan when, all of a sudden, there he was! The image of Willis appeared right before me, "in my face!" "Now we can collaborate!" he announced. He communicated—telepathically—messages for Charlene, his wife, and for Violet, his past assistant, which I later faxed to both.

Willis has continued to "collaborate" with me in this way off and on now for the past few years. The next time he made an appearance was one night when I returned to my room after speaking at the Sacramento Learning Exchange. I decided to check my e-mail briefly, before crawling into bed. It had been a long day.

There was an e-mail from a lady I did not know. She introduced herself, writing that she was a longtime friend of Willis's. Apparently she and his widow were in Seattle at that time, commemorating his birthday. Charlene had expressed interest and appreciation for the message I had sent from Willis. They both wondered if he might want to send them another message on that occasion.

Oh brother, I thought to myself. I was so tired. But sure enough, there was Willis again, showing up right beside me. More accurately described, Willis's thoughts connected to my frequency and I received them clearly, through pictures. Quickly, I typed the message that I received from him. He wanted them both to know that he was there with them. He was laughing about the smell of pungent smoke, a pink sunset, a red rhododendron, and he knew about a special stool. None of this made any sense to me, but then, information for others rarely does.

The next morning there was a response from the woman in Seattle, regarding my message from Willis. "Bingo!" she wrote back. "You got it, right on! We were sitting on a patio, intending to catch the beautiful pink sunset. Our drinks were placed on a little stool from Willis's birthplace that we have here. The view of the sunset was blocked, because the chimney next door had exploded and the smelly smoke was everywhere. Charlene was sitting in front of a red rhododendron!"

Another time, during my yearly trip to London, I was reading a client from India. I had first read him and his British wife when they lived in Switzerland. They would meet me for consultations in London, or when they happened to be in New York City. They had since relocated to London. I was tuning in to various matters in my client's reading, when there he was again! It was Willis! "You knew Willis?" I asked. I had no idea that they had known each other.

"Yes, I knew him very well. I had tremendous respect for him," he said.

"Well, Willis wants you to know that 'the dream you dreamed is true!' He's showing me a scene of some place on a mountain, where people will gather, leaders from all over the world. Visionaries. There's some natural wood and red woven tapestries on the walls in this future place."

"Do you know what Willis is talking about?" I asked, still amazed at the synchronicity.

"Yes, I do. I once hosted a retreat at my villa in the south of France. It was attended by Willis and other 'futurists.' We went into a meditation to dream a dream of the future. Three of us saw the very same future, in detail! That's what Willis is showing you!"

Another time Willis entered into a phone consultation I was doing for a fellow who was putting together a documentary on death and dying. Willis said for him to send his proposal to IONS for funds to assist with the project. He did, and they responded affirmatively.

Willis joined another phone consultation that same year, to convey his love and support to a female colleague—my client—to whom he expressed regret that he had not sufficiently expressed his appreciation when they worked together years before. "I was stuck pretty much in the old traditional male 'think tank' way of operating in business back then. You did so much to assist and support our work when it really mattered!" My client was deeply moved.

So it seems that when Willis expressed his desire to "collaborate" he had an inner, timeless sense of our ability to do that one day. I had no idea it would be from the Other Side.

## REMEMBERING MICHAEL

I picked up an important phone message, just before I took a walk down Sixth Avenue in Manhattan. It was the same afternoon that Willis Harman had "popped in" with his message. The voice said, "We know that you care about Michael. We didn't know if you were aware that he had moved to the Bay Area and is suffering from stomach cancer." It was someone calling from the school in Newport Beach, California, where my children attended from kindergarten to high school.

My thoughts went back to one of the most challenging times of my life, a time that some might call "dark night of the soul." My children were having a terrible time—reacting to the effects of divorce—and overwhelming circumstances left me the designated single parent, the only one there for my kids.

I truly did not know if I was made of the right stuff to make it through. Surrendering to the Source in the darkest moments brought me out of periodic tailspins and gifted me with meaningful synchronicities. Oftentimes, they were my only evidence that God hadn't forgotten me, that I was not alone and was truly being watched over. The rest of my survival depended upon my remembering to breathe, listening to George Winston's music—

which helped me release (by embracing) my fears—and reaching out to a few very special friends.

One of those friends was Michael, my son's beloved fourth-grade teacher. I remember thinking at the time—circumstances tempting me toward cynicism—"Wouldn't you know, it takes a gay man to have that kind of sensitivity!" Indeed, Michael gave Dylan desperately needed attention, tenderness and compassion, like no other.

Michael served as a loving authority figure for Dylan, finding a just balance between necessary chastisement and loving encouragement. Dylan would sit at his desk, continuously fiddling miscellaneous school supplies into eccentric inventions. Michael had a difficult time describing to me, straight-faced, the day that Dylan distracted the entire class from their studies with a roller-coaster-like track, which he'd fashioned from index cards, that efficiently scooted along ball bearings and paper clips—up, down and around an elaborate route.

A few times, Michael took Dylan to Ruby's at the beach, for hamburgers at the end of the pier, when he sensed that Dylan needed a friend. Michael gave more of his time when I needed someone to listen, but he always maintained a very professional, and thereby much more effective, position. I had not seen nor heard from Michael since I moved my children from southern California.

When I returned from my walk, I decided to call the number left for me at the message center. Michael's partner answered, saying that he was not doing well and requested that I call back in one hour, when he'd try to have Michael up and able to talk. That is what I did.

"Michael!" I began. "It's so wonderful to find you. I understand that you're about to begin your next journey."

"Yes," he said, sounding very weak, "I think, maybe, tomorrow."

"Michael, can you feel your mother around you?"

"Sometimes, I think so, but I'm not sure," he answered.

"She's there for you, Michael, she'll be there to help you over. She's laughing about a memory of . . . rug rats?" I said, a bit puzzled.

"Oh," he laughed softly, "that's what she used to call the neighbors' kids."

"Michael," I said, "I hope that this has been a time for you to receive all the love that you've given so freely and generously to people like Dylan and me. You were so kind. The love really came through. Please remember that there is nothing, absolutely nothing to fear. You will go to the Light and feel love like never before."

"Thank you," he said.

"Michael, I love you." I hung up and had a good cry. It was unusual for me to be on this end of things. It was a good reminder of what a majority of my clients are feeling when they call or sit before me.

The next day there was another message for me. Again, it was from the school. I heard the voice of Judy, one of the teachers. She is from England and is a real taskmaster, the kind who works the children very hard and is greatly appreciated by parents and children—later. My children never had a class with her, but she kept an eye out for both of them. She became a dear friend and shared a great appreciation for Michael.

"Louise, we just want you to know that we called up to Michael's yesterday. It happened to be right after you'd called. Michael's partner said how much Michael appreciated your call. Apparently, after he hung up, he went back to bed and never woke up."

I was stunned. I tried to recall the feeling—what I can now define as the "heart-link"—that I felt the day before, when I spoke to Michael. It was a very particular feeling. It was the very same frequency, felt in a very specific place in my heart, that I had felt for Michael ten years before.

Three days later, I felt that feeling again, the very same. It was Michael popping in this time! He appeared, looking handsome, healthy and whole, smiling his radiant smile. He was waving to me and saying, "Thanks. I made it!"

I couldn't believe it. That same feeling. No different from when I felt it ten years before and three days before. It really dramatized to me what that eternal link is. Most definitely it is found in the heart.

Months later, I was having dinner with Dylan, who now lives in Brooklyn and works in Manhattan. He was wrestling with some big decisions in his life. Suddenly I was distracted by a presence beside him. My attention is not usually directed that way when I'm "off duty." It was, unmistakably, Michael! He was still watching over Dylan, like a guide. He smiled and winked at me, saying—telepathically—"He's going to be fine."

## Becoming a Receiver: Pay Attention to Your Dreams

At the beginning of this chapter, you read about Tracy receiving confirmation that she had been reached by a dear friend in her dreams. As an awakened individual, you'll become aware of operating on several levels of consciousness. Your eternal spirit inhabits the physical body that allows you to move around on the stage of your life, and your ego-self gives definition to the character you're playing. Your "light body" travels in and out of its physical experience and physical container; it serves many purposes and benefits from learning in many dimensions. You also meet with souls on the Other Side when you travel this way. Sometimes you'll feel that you were actually visiting with each other at some location. Or you might simply awaken with a clear (or even faint) recollection that you have been together or have spoken with each other.

One of the most useful tools to assist with your expansion is to listen to the unconscious. You can do this by paying attention to your dreams. I have mentioned that it is through your dreams that your subconscious re-presents to you what your heart recorded but your mind rationalized away. Edgar Cayce, "the Sleeping Prophet," a renowned psychic and teacher, received his healing information in a sleep state. He was able to hold both a conscious and unconscious level of awareness simultaneously. Here are some of his ideas about the power of dream work:

- "Anything we might wish to know, we can safely obtain through dreams."
- "Dreams are not only for information, but for actual transforming experiences."
- "Nothing of significance in our lives occurs without being first previewed in our dream world."
- "The only time a dream is understood is when it is applied."

I'm amazed at how my dreams give me a deeper understanding of the issues I'm processing at any given time in my life, issues that are catalyzed by situations and events that come upon my path. Sometimes I assume that I'm wrestling with a particular repeating theme, but my dreams show me something different and open me up to greater possibilities for healing.

Dream interpretation is fun and fascinating. Your unconscious is a delightful punster and delivers images and symbols that go beyond time. It will take you back to your past, revealing and confirming that certain events—and emotional reactions to them—did occur. Your child-self needs that validation. It's the only way that you will be able to trust what you feel in the present. You must be able to trust feelings in the present, in order to trust intuitive sensings.

I've noticed that I tend to remember my dreams more vividly when I'm on the road, traveling with my work. I suspect that this is because at those times, I wake up in physical surroundings that differ from my home environment. The familiar cues to which I usually awaken at home pull me into my day so expediently—reminding me of my life and the day ahead—that I'm pulled too quickly to "catch" the dream. It takes practice and conscious commitment to allow yourself the time to awaken more slowly, stay in neutral and register the dream.

Taking the few moments to record the dream at that moment will help you create the new habit. It takes practice, and the more you take time to remember, the more frequently—and vividly—you'll begin to retrieve your dreams. One friend writes a note to her "dream fairies" at night and places it under her pillow. She writes her request for insightful information to assist her with a current, specific issue. This helps to program your unconscious subconscious with the suggestion that you are one who remembers your dreams, and it will position you to be receptive to receiving and remembering them.

Keep a dream diary of deceased loved ones' appearances in dreams. How did they appear to you? Were you in a particular location? Were you in present time, or in the past? Were you having a conversation, or was it just a "knowing" of their presence? Did they communicate in symbols or actual words? Did they show you a memory from the past, or give you a message? Try to remember what your thoughts were before you dropped off to sleep on those occasions. Is there a pattern? Write a letter describing those visits to yourself.

Tonight, write a note to your dream fairies, requesting insightful information on any aspect of your life. Or just "ask to be shown" what you need to know. (Don't forget to add, "gently!") If you request a visit from a loved one, don't forget what they often advise: "Let your last thoughts before sleep be those of gratitude. They open the heart and create the frequency that lets us come through more clearly." This creates the heart-link.

Keep a notebook or tape recorder by your bed to record your dream the moment you have retrieved it upon awakening. Gift yourself with the first five, quiet moments of your day to lie in bed and retrieve your dream before rushing to start your day.

# CHAPTER SIX

# Soul Agreements

*S*oul agreements are made by individuals or groups prior to entering into a lifetime on earth. As with most "plans" we make from the wider perspective that is available while we are still in spirit, most of us forget our agreements once we are in a body again and we end up living our lives to the best of our abilities.

I have the privilege and the advantage of viewing clients' lives in the context of a much bigger picture. My perspective can help them understand the meaning of circumstances in their lives in a more purposeful, meaningful way. Some peoples' paths seem to invite what they feel is uncaring, outrageous fortune. Through my clairvoyant viewfinder, I can see a perfect plan, incredibly configured to carry out a soul's chosen mission.

We are schooled to view life in this dimension from a very limited, linear perspective. From that perspective, we perceive that life is cheating us when loved ones are taken away "before their time." When we are able to view events from a wider perspective, we often find that in the bigger picture, it was indeed their time. In countless consultations, I receive information that the departure of a loved one is "right on schedule," in spite of the shock, pain and grief that has resulted among those remaining on this plane.

Sometimes I discover a sort of "pact" that exists among a group of souls who have agreed to return together in order to complete unfinished business or to reunite and assist in each other's growth in this journey. The following stories are examples of such soul agreements. The first includes a profound analogy relating to our erroneous perception of death. The second account involved an entire neighborhood. The third recounts a beautiful unfolding of events in the last hours of my client's mother's life, so configured as to lead one to suspect a previous agreement.

## LOCKED OUTSIDE THE BACKDOOR

*We experience our lives within time and space. Our normal or usual relationship to time is linear and sequential; events occur one at a time, one after another. We relate to our world in terms of our physicality—our physically embodied selves—placed some "where," at some physical location.*

*Not so, on the Other Side, beyond this dimension—contrary to what we have been taught to believe. Most of us have learned that we go to some "place"—usually understood as a heaven ("up there") or a hell ("down there").*

*I believe it is this view—that we go to some "place" when we leave our physical bodies—that creates such an overwhelming sense of loss when a loved one dies. If indeed they aren't "dead" even though buried in the ground, then they must be some "place," so very far away.*

*The new emerging awareness about the death of the body includes the concept that when we die, we simply make our transition into a nonphysical "space" or dimension; in other words, we vacate the physical premises. Moving between our "real" world and the world of spirit is a little like the process affiliated with desktop publishing. You click a menu to choose "bring to front" or "send to back." This allows you to move around layers of graphics or information.*

*When I "tune in" to the frequency of loved ones, in a flash— just a thought away—there they are. They simply "come forward," and then I proceed. We each adjust our frequencies for better reception, just like tuning a radio.*

*I do the same frequency fine tuning with my clients, whether I am with them in person or talking with them from any location in the world. Again, our energy is "nonlocal." More easily than modern communication technology allows us to send (and receive) electronic signals around the world, our individual energy fields can send (and receive) frequencies anywhere in this physical dimension—and anywhere in the nonphysical dimension.*

*The following account underlines the misperception that a loved one is some place far away. Our work together helped my client to understand that the heart connection linking her to her daughter had allowed them to be many things to each other over numerous incarnations.*

I first read Barbara several years ago, shortly after she lost her six-year-old daughter to a brain tumor. Kate presented herself immediately in Barbara's initial consultation, bathed in beautiful light, projecting herself as the little girl her mother grieved for.

Kate looked radiant and happy. She began as most loved ones do, showing me scenes that specify where they have been in touch since passing. This validated an intuitive sensing Barbara had felt at certain times, knowing that Kate was near.

Kate said that she and her mother had lost and found each other in several other lifetimes. She showed me scenes of herself as an old woman, when she'd been Barbara's mother; then, posing in a military uniform, when they were buddies in a war (both men); and then, scenes of a very religious, monastic lifetime they spent together in an abbey.

Kate said, "It is in this lifetime that we're playing out the spiritual truths that we both came in knowing and supporting in each other." Kate was so pleased with all the peoples' lives that had been deeply touched and awakened by her "death."

She told Barbara that this was the plan, and that she was proud of her mom for the wonderful influence she would be to others in the future, helping them to overcome their fear of death. Kate sympathized with her mother's grief, and said that when Barbara eventually moved through the pain, they would be in touch in a "new way."

By the time I last read Barbara, she was receiving clear communications from Kate each day, during her morning shower. She plans to compile the messages into a book. It was in this consultation that Kate sent a poignant message: Kate showed me a scene of a little girl standing in the backyard of a house. She had been locked outside the backdoor.

"You never did that to her, did you?" I asked.

"No," Barbara replied. "That was me, when I was little."

"Oh," I said, pausing, "Kate seems to know that. She is saying, 'That's how WE feel when YOU believe that WE'RE DEAD!'"

What a graphic reminder of the false ideas we hold in our minds about the "death" of loved ones. They have not gone to some "place" up or down, nor have they left anything behind, except family and friends who miss their physical presence. They have simply slipped into the nonphysical dimension, as we all will one day. They are not—and will not be—dead and buried in the ground. They are, as we will be one day, only a thought away.

## THE WAGON PARTY

I first spoke with Louise after the death of my close friend and next-door neighbor, Chelsea. My husband had met Louise several years earlier and, for some reason, I felt she had something important to communicate to me after the traumatic experience of Chelsea's death. I called Louise and she did in fact have much information to communicate to me about what had transpired at the time of Chelsea's death and about my relationship to her.

I was with Chelsea when she died. We were next-door neighbors and had become friends ten months earlier when we bought our houses and moved in at the same time. Chelsea became ill in June of 1995 and I was very concerned about her health. Five days into her illness, I took her back to a walk-in clinic where she had received care in the preceding days. Within six hours, Chelsea was gone from our world at the young age of thirty. This sudden and inexplicable death shocked me and all who knew Chelsea, especially our neighbors who witnessed her sudden illness and death.

The first thing Louise shared with me was that I was returning a favor Chelsea had done for me in another lifetime. I had apparently died in her arms during a lifetime in which we were traveling across the country together. Chelsea had messages for me and others, which were communicated through Louise: most importantly that she had gone to the Light and that the prayers of all those around her had made her transition easier.

She was concerned for her husband and her two-year-old daughter, and she relayed some information about how she could be communicated with now that she was no longer in her body. While in physical form, she loved her garden and its beautiful flowers. It seems she was in heaven in her garden now, at peace and watching over those of us still in our earthly bodies, acting as an angel when we need her.

After I had my initial reading with Louise over the phone, we had the pleasure of having her to our home to meet people from the neighborhood. Many of the people in our cul-de-sac had readings and it became apparent to Louise that we were a "soul group." We had been together in other lifetimes and were reunited in this lifetime to do special work involving spiritual enlightenment.

On the evening of our group session, Louise was able to interpret for Chelsea, and some remarkable things occurred. She was able to pick up on Chelsea's personal language and gestures in a way that ascertained for all of us that she was indeed present with us in the room, in spirit form. She also relayed that she was wearing a black velvet dress and had her hair done up especially for our communication. Bob, Chelsea's husband, and I were shocked. Six months before, Chelsea and Bob had posed in front of my fireplace for Christmas pictures before they went to his company's Christmas party. She had worn a black dress and had her hair especially done for the occasion.

The inner connectedness of our group was remarkable. We were able to identify some of the positions we had had in the group in previous lifetimes. We thought it was remarkable that Louise had seen us in a pioneer lifetime when we were traveling across the country in a wagon train.

Circling the wagons back in that lifetime was parallel to our current configurations on our horseshoe-shaped cul-de-sac. The information Louise imparted to us was confirming in the sense that she assured us that we had indeed been together before, and with our incredible closeness and friendships, we could feel and connect on a very deep "soul" level.

The enlightenment we gained through the extraordinary experience of Chelsea's passing served as a wake-up call for many people who knew Chelsea well, and especially for the people who live on our street. Our world changed forever on the day Chelsea left the physical plane. But through time we came to a better understanding of the game of life—and the illusion of our lives here in the material world. Chelsea brought us this enlightenment, and it was Louise who first deciphered it for us.

*Heather Kelly*


## PARTICIPATING IN THE PROCESS

Losing my mother was the most devastating experience of my life. No other event can come close to the searing pain of emptiness that split my heart and still reduces me to tears when I relate the experience. I thought I could never come to grips with this loss.

Two months after my mother's passing, I took the opportunity to have a consultation with Louise Hauck. As I expected, Louise connected with my mother, who was excited to let me know that all I had shared with her before her death, she was indeed now experiencing. Before her death, I had read to her from several books that recounted conversations between those who had passed on and those who were still in the body.

My mother was a skeptic. I never knew until this moment that what I had shared made an impression and created an opening for her next journey. Louise asked me, "What do bows mean to you? Your mother is showing me a bow, wanting to thank you!" I completely broke into tears, knowing that it was undeniably my mother who was speaking.

I had designed, produced and sent to friends and family eighty tributes to my mother, on each of which I tied a chiffon bow. I had been making cards for my mother since I was eight and she had kept every one of them. I hated the impersonal announcement cards that funeral homes provided and I thought she deserved a more personal, loving tribute to her life.

My mother continued to speak to me through Louise. She thanked me for the light that I sent to her in her room the night she died. She said that it opened a space wherein loving spirits entered to help her across to the Other Side. I was stunned. No one else but my mother could have known this.

I had not shared what I had done with anyone, including my sister, who was with me in the hospital room that night. My sister and I had kept a vigil over my mother since her admittance to the hospital. The doctors, according to her wishes, had not attached oxygen or given any form of life support to help her. Just as we were going to leave to go home and get a little sleep, my sister picked up the chart at the foot of Mother's bed.

She noticed that the nurses had recorded an irregular heartbeat. That was enough for us to change our plans, requesting lounge chairs to stay the night in her room. We settled in, and my sister read while I meditated to quiet myself. Then I prayed that Mother would pass in peace. I was inches from my mother's face and though I longed to reach out and stroke her hair, I held back, knowing instinctively that she would try to stay with us if I did. I knew that she wanted to leave.

Feeling guided, I visualized a bright light coming straight down from God and through the crown of my head. I added all the love I had ever felt for my mother to that light. Then, visualizing a beam going from me to my mother, I surrounded her with love. I saw it as a light filled with a green glow, almost like a laser beam. With my thoughts traveling across this beam, I told her that it was okay for her to leave; we would be fine.

Suddenly my sister looked up at me with a smile and we both felt this inexplicable rush of joy brush past us. Before we could speak, both of us turned to Mother and realized she had gone. There was a moment when we just sat there transfixed, after which we got up, kissed her and hugged each other before going out to tell the nurses she had died.

Louise brought that moment back to me in an instant with my mother's words. That is when I understood exactly what had happened that night. It was more than just a prayer, more than a meditation. It was a communion of love between those of us in the body and those in the spirit. It was an invocation to God and loving spirits, waiting to come forward and enter into that space to make Mother's passing more peaceful.

Louise continued with the communication, asking me if I wanted to know what my mother was doing now. I nodded yes, and she began to describe a crystal-lit hallway, resembling a school, where a door was opening and spirits were asking my mother to come and join them.

Louise asked me if Mother had tended to be a bit self-effacing. Again, I nodded yes. She continued to tell me that when these spirits asked Mother to come join them she felt so much love and acceptance from them that she was sure they had made a mistake; they couldn't possibly be talking to her.

Through Louise, she went on to describe peaceful gardens where she sat contemplating and other classrooms where she was learning the true meaning of love. She was learning to love herself again. She told me that she was so excited to be a part of this communicating between the two dimensions and that I should not see her as sick and in pain. She had put that away.

She told me she had no regrets. It was on that small statement, "she had no regrets," that I began to build the foundation for a new way to remember her, a new way to communicate with her, a new way to see my own passing when the time came. Through Louise and the communication with my mother, I found a way to overcome the sadness, to harness the bond and the love that tied us so deeply together in this life. Now I was determined to use it to help others who fear dying and death.

My mother said that we would be working together again. Here we are, together, recounting her own passing so that in some small way this might influence others to look through their fears and their sadness to the glorious awareness that the life of the spirit is everlasting.

*CJ Conner*

## Becoming a Receiver: Meditate

It was only through meditating that CJ was able to receive the guidance—the answers to her prayers—that enabled her to facilitate her mother's transition into the nonphysical dimension. You must be able to quiet your active mind in order to hear the messages that will come to you and to eventually "transcend," that is, go to a deeper level of perception and understanding that will take you beyond your understanding of this physical, linearly perceived dimension.

There are excellent meditation tapes available that can guide you through sensory and visual imagery, or methods that encourage you to hold a mantra, a special word, in your consciousness. When you hold that word in your thoughts, your mind cannot engage in busy thoughts that distract you from a peaceful, deeper level. In a sense, you're giving the "chattering monkey" (your mind) a "banana."

The effects of meditation are cumulative. Twenty minutes per day is ideal. Eventually you transcend from the noisy mind to the quiet stillness where you rest or gain insights at a deep level, or experience expanded consciousness, where all is known and you experience your connection to all that is. I've reached a point now where I instantly "go there" when I meditate. I call it "checking in with headquarters." After twenty minutes, I come back in, refreshed and regenerated, often with increased clarity or new insights.

Each of us will find our own way to tap the unlimited source of information by asking that we receive what is for our highest good and being open to the new ways of "seeing" and sensing.

―――――――――― **TRY THIS** ――――――――――

Take the phone off the hook. Turn off your fax, your cell phone, your computer. Take yourself to a quiet place, ideally to your sacred space. Sit comfortably with your feet on the floor, your hands in your lap, palms upward (a receptive posture). Surround yourself with the Light. Take a deep, cleansing breath, slowly inhaling, feeling your lungs gently fill with air. Then exhale, slowly. Now, stretch out all over—arms and hands, legs and feet—and expand your chest cavity. Stretch your jaw and neck, roll your head from side to side.

Now relax, slowly, from head to toe. Notice where you're holding tension. Gently direct your attention there, then relax into that area and release, gently, easily.

Now make sure your spine is straight but relaxed. Take another deep breath, slowly inhaling. Then exhale slowly, this time allowing all your limiting beliefs, negative thoughts or worries to leave you, floating out on that breath. Continue to sit quietly. Think the word "heart," "peace" or "love" or another word that is meaningful to you. Just bring the word into your awareness effortlessly, and repeat it slowly, gently, in your mind.

Observe when your thoughts take you away from your word. They might divert you to thoughts about all that you need to accomplish in this day. Gently come back to your word, repeating it slowly, gently. Continue to observe the thoughts that take you elsewhere, then come back to your word again, repeating it slowly and effortlessly. Do this for one week for twenty minutes each sitting, at the same time each day. That will be your meditation time. Taking the time to do this each day will quiet you. You will notice that as you become more relaxed and centered, you'll actually have more time to accomplish other things. And you'll be more present in each moment.

# CHAPTER SEVEN

# Skeptics

*I*'m often asked if there are people who I am unable to read. While I always receive information, there are two types of consultations that can be the most frustrating for me. The first involves sessions with very analytical people, who can only think in logical, literal terms. They are unable to understand the interpretation of symbols and images. For example, once during a consultation, I was looking into the childhood of the man I was reading. "I see that there was an Aunt Rose, who made raspberry Jell-O," I said. This was significant, because my client had been abandoned by his parents at a young age and was raised by his Aunt Rose. He looked perplexed, responding, "Didn't everyone have an Aunt Rose who made raspberry Jell-O?" That was the only way he could logically understand that I could know this information from his past.

The second type of frustrating consultations are those with clients who have very specific expectations about what they hope to receive in the consultation. Often quite skeptical, their determination to test me—and to hear what they want to hear as proof—prevents them from hearing all the information that I'm attempting to interpret for them. This is why I strongly urge them to go back later and listen to their taped session. They often hear meaningful messages or evidence that rings true, that they couldn't have begun to hear in the consultation. Additionally, some of the information won't make sense—or be revealed—until a later time.

The following story is a wonderful example of both: a consultation with a very analytical, skeptical person with specific expectations. Each time she listened to her tape after a session, she would kick herself, wondering how she could have missed so much specific and relevant information at the time. She would then schedule another reading, vowing, "This time I'm going to just shut up!"

## SNOWMAN POOP

*After a few sessions, my client started to feel—and trust—a very new, different kind of sensing that circumvented her busy mind. She became more comfortable with a feeling that began to override her logical thinking. She started to understand how I see images and symbols, and my efforts to interpret them as best I can. At this time, she has actually become an apprentice, and is doing very well in our periodic sessions over the phone. She has come a long way since our first session.*

*There was only one time in that first consultation when she did not respond with, "Yes, but didn't everybody . . . such and such?" After identifying Denny, her husband, who had recently made his transition, I said, "He is showing me something like a charm bracelet, or a necklace with something hung on it, on the necklace."*

"Yes, but don't most women have a necklace with something dangling from it?"

"Is there something special about what's dangling from this necklace?"

"Well, yes . . ."

"Okay, that's what he's talking about."

"But what's he saying about it? It's very specific . . . if you could just . . ."

Exasperated, I said, "Okay, believe it or not, not everybody has a charm bracelet, or a charm on a necklace. He's trying as hard as he can to give you the specifics and I'm just the interpreter, okay? A charm doesn't mean anything to you?"

"Well, actually it does! It's the Christmas gift I gave him, the month before he passed. I had a charm of a cabin put on a necklace that was engraved with, 'Home is where YOU are.' I did this because we were having to put our home on the market to pay for alternative treatment, not covered by insurance. I wanted him to know that I didn't care. That HE was what mattered. Then after he passed, I added his wedding band to the necklace. I've been wearing it ever since."

Later she told me, "I knew the second you mentioned 'charm' that it had to be him, but I was wanting you to tell me all the details, more than HE was showing YOU. HE knew that the charm part should do it—and it did, in my heart—but I still wanted to test you. I was not completely 'getting it,' that you were able to give me only what he gave to you!"

Later in her consultation, I asked if she had a basement. She said that she did. I told her that I saw an animal going down the stairs. "That just happened this morning! Our dog broke through the gate barrier at the top of the stairs. She's had recent surgery and isn't supposed to climb stairs. Denny's computer is *down there. She was looking for him." She was responding so much more receptively now. She continued, "I don't know the password to the computer!"*

*"He's saying it's 'from cabin.'"*

*"Yes," she agreed, adding, "maybe it's an anagram of the word 'cabin'! I think he did that once before!"*

*The next session began with Denny showing me a scene of him standing behind his wife, who sat at the computer. It looked like he was whispering something in her ear. He was laughing.*

*"Yes!" she said, sounding quite excited. "I found the password! I tried the word 'cabin,' but something told me to reverse the two middle letters. That was the password! I found it!"*

*I laughed, loving how it all makes so much sense in the bigger picture. "That was Denny there with you. He was giving you the password!"*

*This story also demonstrates that sometimes, when we think we need to ask forgiveness from another, the issue is more our own need to forgive ourselves. It's also a lovely example of how supportive a loved one can be—from the Other Side—assisting with the healing of the one left behind.*

My beloved husband, Denny, was diagnosed with cancer on Christmas Eve 1997. He had been having painful sinus headaches daily since October. The doctor put him on antibiotics and by Thanksgiving, he had lost his voice. His wonderful voice. The doctor still insisted it was sinuses, so I made an appointment with an ear, nose and throat specialist. He did a bronchoscopy but wasn't going to take a chest X-ray until we specifically requested it. That's when the tumor was found. They "gave" him two years to live.

In January 1998 Denny was very ill, thin, with no energy at all. By June he was greatly improved, having gained weight, and he felt good. We took many day trips during the summer and had a great time. His voice almost returned to normal.

Then in October, his headaches started again. He passed over on January 25, 1999. I was devastated! Even though he was diagnosed as terminal, we thought he had turned it around. So it still came as a shock. We had been together twenty-seven years. I didn't want to go on without him, but suicide wasn't an option. I believe that I would just have to come back and go through it all again. No, I knew I would have to stay in this physical body and finish whatever it is I came to do. But I didn't know how.

What added to the awfulness of it was the fact that I felt Denny was angry with me before he passed. Three weeks later I connected with Louise for a reading. I told her nothing about Denny's passing, expecting to get a standard reading. She started with the life progression—finding a point in my life and moving it forward and backward. At another time I would have welcomed this kind of information, but I was anxiously waiting for her to mention Denny.

Testing her, I didn't want to give Louise any information she could feed back to me. I was being so skeptical, even when I was desperate to connect with Denny so we could "make up." I needed to know that he was doing okay, that he was comfortable and happy. I believed he probably was, but I wanted to hear it from him.

During this first reading, I didn't quite "get" how Louise was receiving the information. I'd get excited from the information, then turn right around and wonder why she didn't get other information or get it in a certain way. This could best be explained by adding a portion of the reading here, where Denny comes through. It's interesting that earlier, in the life progression, Louise mentioned my need to heal a tendency to internalize and blame myself for everything.

Louise: "Have you lost a friend?"

Darsi: "I just lost my husband."

L: "Okay, your husband is here. There is a "D" and an "R" around him."

D: "Yes." (crying)

L: "Dick or Richard, or what?"

D: "Dennis Robert."

L: "Oh, that's him! He's D-R, right?"

D: "Yes"

L: "Okay, no wonder I said when we first started, that you're feeling in retreat and hesitant to get back out there."

D: "It just happened three weeks ago. That's why I wanted to connect with you."

L: "Okay, all right, so I wanted to lay some groundwork for the bigger picture, to see what you're becoming and how you've been challenged."

D: "A lot of what you've said, like you're talking about my life—in the progression—it's like I was playing out all the same themes, condensed into my life with him!"

L: "Okay, your life with him, great. Okay."

D: "It's interesting, because you didn't know and so you were talking about our life."

L: "Well, I knew there was someone on the Other Side who wanted to come through."

D: "Oh, God! I hope so!"

L: "Oh, yes! Well, that's where I got the D-R. Okay, so I wanted to lay some groundwork. It's wonderful that you can see everything I've been saying about your life's challenges, represented in the context of your marriage. It was a bit of a microcosm of your life in general, wasn't it?"

D: "Yes, exactly."

L: "Okay, now he's saying that . . ."

D: "Is he really—are you connecting with him?"

L: "Well, where do you think I got the D-R?"

D: "Well, maybe from my mind."

L: "No, he's right here!"

D: "I wanted . . . I was hoping . . . because I thought maybe he was mad at me when he passed." (sob, sob)

L: "No, no, no, no."

D: " . . . and that's why I needed to connect."

L: "No, no, no. He wants to give you some examples of when he's been around you, to help you trust those sensations."

D: "Oh, good . . ."

L: "Denny is sending me the scent of roses—does that make any sense?"

D: "Well, yes, a friend brought a bunch of roses by the house the day he passed."

L: "Okay." He wants you to know that he was right there, beside you."

D: "Oh, God . . ." (But to myself I was thinking, this could apply to anybody!)

L: "Now see, loved ones aren't far away, in some place . . ."

D: "I believe this, Louise . . . I know . . . I've even been reading a book recently where people have connected with their loved ones and I think, "I want to connect with Denny, to know if he's still mad at me, if he does know how much I love him. Is he okay? That's what I need to know."

L: "Well, that's what he's here to help you with . . ."

D: "He's not mad at me?"

L: "No!"

D: "In the last hours, he got mad at me. I want him to know how sorry I am . . ."

L: "No, no. What he sees is the whole life together and . . ."

D: "I was counting on that. I had a feeling that's what he would do and I should trust that he would not be that petty . . ."

L: "Okay, now let me tell you something. What you have to heal about those last hours—that you have some fear about—is representative of something else that is repeating from your past. I'm sensing that your guilt about the end with Denny is reminiscent of something from your childhood."

D: "Why? Because I . . ."

L: "Wait! Let me finish! Were you at your mother's or grandmother's deathbed? Was someone angry at you just before they died?"

D: "My grandmother. See, I was just a kid and I wanted to spend the night at a friend's house. She said, NO! I did it anyway."

L: "So, that's what Denny is wanting to help you see! That little girl inside you is projecting all the guilt that you felt with the grandmother. Denny is saying, 'It has nothing to do with us.'"

D: "But, why not, because I was . . ."

L: "This came up again to dramatize for you the guilt that you're carrying that needs to be . . ."

D: "But, I was not . . . I mean . . ."

L: "Let me finish. That whole scenario with Denny was staged for your growth. To amplify a burden that you've been carrying. This causes you to distrust yourself and makes it hard for you to trust others. The Universe is trying to help you heal.

"I have a friend who was caring for her mother who was ill with the Hong Kong flu. She left the room to get something for her mother, who died in those few moments that her daughter was absent from the room. The incident triggered a very codependent tendency— a strong feeling that she has to rescue everyone—that has challenged her for years. She used to be terrified to leave anyone in pain or in need. They could die! Years later, she discovered this in therapy. This revelation has helped to awaken her and make her more attentive to setting personal 'boundaries' for herself.

"So, Denny wants you to know that your fear about the anger at the end had more to do with you and your grandmother than it did with you and him. He really wants you to know that.

"Now, he's showing me some other scenes. One of you, talking to him in a picture. He says that he hears every word."

D: "OOH, I have been! Looking him right in the eyes . . . "

(Again I felt doubtful, even though it felt right on. My mind kicked in with, "But anybody would in this situation . . . I wish she'd be more specific . . .")

L: "OK, that's what he's talking about; he's saying, "I'm there; I hear every word."

D: "I want to connect with him . . ."

L: "That's why he's doing this here today; he's giving you examples of when he's there and he's wanting to help you trust the feeling."

D: "Oh, I hope this is for real; this would . . . but why did he leave?"

(I was still questioning this, because I was still thinking I could/should have done more.)

L: "Now, he's showing me some more memories. There's something about, something round and white, like a softball, or marshmallows. Does that ring a bell? Any memory? I never know if it's a message or a memory."

D: "Well, there are cotton balls around here, but I don't know why he'd be showing them."

(Wow! I wanted more specific confirmation, here it is, but I didn't get it at the time!)

L: "There wasn't any memory about roasting marshmallows, or . . ."

D: "Well, yes, but anybody has that . . ."

L: "Not necessarily. See, that's your mind coming in, trying to get rational about this."

D: "Well, we did roast marshmallows out there at the fire pit, but . . ."

(I wasn't buying this, too generic, even though it was appropriate, as we did use the fire pit at the cabin frequently and always roasted marshmallows. What came up for me later, after the reading, was something very specific about marshmallows: The month before Denny's passing, we went to a craft show and bought a little joke-gift, a small baggie filled with marshmallows that had a little note card attached, saying: "You've been bad/so here's the scoop—all you get/is snowman poop!" It is amazing that I was so in my rational mind that I couldn't identify that in the reading.)

> L: "Was there some memory about tying a tie or scarf around someone's neck?"
> D: "No, I don't remember any . . ."
> L: "Do you like to wear scarves?"
> D: "No."
> L: "Did you help him tie his tie?"
> D: "No."
> L: "This might come to you later; something about something being draped around the neck, wrapping something around someone's neck."

(I asked for specifics, and here's another one that she gave me! But I didn't get it until later. I still wasn't tuned in to how Louise receives information, how she tries to interpret it. I completely missed this one. I had crocheted a scarf for Denny in 1975, and he was still wearing it up to the month he passed!)

> L: "Was there a memory about a wheel—with spokes?"
> D: "No."

(Yes! It was a big deal that Denny got to feeling so much better that he was able to ride a bike.)

L: "Did he used to get headaches?"

D: "He had some . . ."

L: ". . . and when he got ill, was it something in the head?"

D: "Well, no . . ."

L: "He's talking about when his head would get tight. Did he used to . . ."

D: "Well, yes! He did. Well, of course, sinuses were part . . . that's how it all started.

(Finally, I get it! I was so focused on his passing of lung cancer, which I expected her to say, that I almost missed this. It was paramount to his suffering! The headaches were the worst for him.)

L: "Okay, that's what it is."

D: "Yes, it started with sinuses and terrible headaches everyday—yes!"

L: "He's saying, 'It's so good to be free of that, to be out of the body; and he's saying that your prayers helped him go to the Light. He's saying that it's sometimes hard to reach you because you're being so hard on yourself and your mind is wanting to understand where he is. But your heart knows."

D: "I believe he's right here. It's not that . . ."

L: "He just wants to help you trust it. He's showing me something about carrots."

D: "Oh, yes! Lots of carrot juice."

(It was a daily treatment, plus we gave them to our dogs as a treat.)

> L: "He's laughing about that."
> D: "He's really happy? Does he miss me? Why did he leave? Couldn't he have stayed longer? Why did he leave so young?"

(I'm still aching here, thinking I could/should have done more. Louise's progression for me was right on, my trying to be everything to everybody. I couldn't shake the feeling that if I'd done better somehow, he wouldn't have died of cancer.)

> L: "He's saying he had a shorter tour of duty—was he ever in the military?"
> D: "Just briefly—a short tour . . ."
> L: "Well, he's using this as a pun. He's showing me himself in a uniform, but he's saying symbolically that he had a shorter tour of duty this lifetime. It was 'time to go back to the drawing board.'"
> D: "So he finished what he came to do?"
> L: "Yes, and he's saying he didn't get to be who he wanted to be spiritually. He's saying you'll know him in another way when he's back, eventually. Not right away. There will be something about the way a child will hold your hand. Denny says, 'You'll know me.' He knows that you'll recognize him. It will be unmistakable. He'll also hope to deal with more of his creativity—which is divine energy expressing itself—and he's saying that you really tried to help him to open up to a new, more sensitive part of himself. He'll want more of that, the next time.

"Now, Denny is showing me a Christmas tree, or something on top of a tree. Is there some memory or joke
about that?"

D: "No."

(I missed another excellent one here because I got hung up on
the "joke" part. No, there was no joke, but there was a wonderful memory. Denny and an owl communicated for thirty
minutes up at our cabin one time. The owl was perched on top
of a pine tree right by the cabin and started hooting. Denny
would mimic the owl. They went on for thirty minutes, the owl
looking right at him. It was wonderful.)

L: "I'll just keep it coming. You can think about it later.
Something now, about opening up a cupboard and
something falling out?"

D: "Absolutely! Several times shortly before he passed."

L: "Anyone named Arthur, or Art?"

D: "Yes!"

L: "And has he been helpful?"

D: "Yes."

L: "Okay, so Denny's saying, 'Open up to the love
around you. I'm just right there. And stop beating
yourself up about the last moments and feeling
responsible for everything that happens."

D: "Was he happy enough with me? Was I too bitchy?
Oh, darn, there's my little kid coming in . . . You know,
part of me watches me do this and I know it's irra-
tional, but I still have those feelings that if I had been
sweeter and nicer and all this other STUFF . . ."

L: "So, Darsi, that's simply what's needing to be healed in you; so just open up the Source and say, 'Show me what I need to know; give me road signs; lead me out of this!' And don't forget to add, 'Clearly and gently!'"

D: "So, he's okay and already doing things?"

L: "Yes, he's in class. Did he used to have some fascination with the stars, the night sky, or . . ."

D: "Oh, yes, he did!"

L: "He's saying he's really able to learn about this now and also about other dimensions and other galaxies."

D: "Oh, that makes me happy!"

(Denny and I used to have wonderful conversations about these topics and spent much time at the cabin looking at the night sky.)

L: "He's fascinated by it all and he's saying, 'A star in the sky . . .' Sometimes, do you see a star in the sky and talk to him?"

D: "Oh, yes . . ."

L: "Again, he says, he's right there beside you. But when you eventually miss less his physical self, when you feel like you're moving through the pain, you're not betraying him or abandoning him. He's saying—as souls often say—'When you miss less the physical me, you're going to start to know the eternal me.'"

I am now more able to trust that there wasn't anything I could have done to change anything. It was his time. And, yes, it's painful for me without his physical presence, missing the life we had together. But it's all right now because I know we're still connected. I know all's well with him and the love is still there. I am better able, now, to trust this connection to my beloved husband and to turn to the Source/God for guidance.

Thanks to readings like these, I'm reminded that we do have an "assignment" when we enter the physical. We might as well get on with it. There's a reason for this painful loss. When I'm back "home" with Denny, I'll be glad I stuck it out and made the best of it!

Now, participating in Louise's apprenticeship program over the phone, I'm beginning to open up to my own intuitive abilities, which are getting easier to trust. I am really surprising myself! I never gave myself enough credit. Seeing the results of this work gives me high hopes.

*Darsi Vanatta*

## INSTRUCTIONS FROM AN ENVIRONMENTAL BIOLOGIST

I am a staunch supporter of the tenets of science. Throughout my life, my philosophical beliefs have been based upon the notion that only phenomena that are observable should be accepted as fact. The majority of scientific disciplines rely upon the accumulation and interpretation of physical or empirical data. Therefore, the concept of an afterlife or the continued existence of the spirit seemed unlikely, if not impossible, because such a notion lies beyond the realm of physical proof. My meeting with Louise, however, began to open my mind to a new line of reasoning. This reasoning serves, at least for myself, to utilize some essential scientific principles in explaining the possible continuation of spiritual energy. My outlook since the consultation has changed enormously.

The meeting with Louise was not something that I would have sought on my own, for I have always been extremely skeptical of things of a supernatural nature. My mother had been referred to Louise through a coworker who thought that an experience of this nature might help to eliminate some of the pain that she was dealing with following my father's youthful passing. Mom hadn't even planned to tell me that she was considering this option, but we have always been very close and, given time, tend to share everything. I encouraged her to go because I was desperate to see her find some type of comfort amidst her grief. I also insisted that I take her because I knew that it would be a very taxing time emotionally, and I did not want her to be alone. I remained skeptical (although admittedly a bit curious) and decided that I would wait outside while the session was under way.

As the consultation began, Louise coaxed me inside for what she explained to be the preamble to the process so that I might have an understanding of my mother's experience that day. She offered background on herself and her gift, and proceeded to relate the experiences of some of her past clients. None of what was being presented to me fit my preconceived notions of the universe, and I was beginning to feel somewhat uncomfortable. Still trying to play the role of the good open-minded scientist as well as the good son, I allowed Louise to persuade me to stay.

What followed was startling. Louise immediately diverged from the topic of my father and asked my mom if her mother had passed. In fact, my grandmother had passed away several years prior. Louise said that my grandmother was there, with her hand on my mother's shoulder. What startled me was the description of my grandmother that Louise offered. She saw her with an apron. This may well refer to an apron that I still envision when conjuring forth images of my grandmother: an apron that my mother still has to this day. Louise asked if she had liked to bake. Well, all of the children in the family had known of her as Grandma Cookie and had typically relished the thought of a visit for her wonderful baking. Now these are characteristics that may be common to many grandmothers from this era, but Louise had certainly gotten my undivided attention at this point.

As anxious as I was to disregard this last exchange as mere chance, the connections did not stop there. Curiously enough, Louise expressed images of the life that my mother and I had experienced since my father's death. Louise inquired about recent images of straightening a picture, another of a picture hanging by a mirror and yet another of a recently planted garden dedicated to Dad. Before leaving for the consultation that morning, a picture of my father had fallen over for no apparent reason, forcing my mother to correct it in distress. I had completed my ritual of acknowledging my dad in his obituary picture hung below a mirror in the dining room. As well, my mother had spent time completing a new garden in the yard with a stone inscribed with the words "DAD'S GARDEN" placed in the center. "He was there, he knows," was the reply from Louise as we described how her images had fit into our lives.

Names that had been pertinent to my father's life just prior to his death began to emerge. Throughout the course of a lifetime, a person can acquire a tremendous pool of acquaintances with many names to choose from, but what seemed uncanny was Louise's ability to relate these names in the proper context. The names of colleagues with whom my father had left unfinished business through his passing were mentioned in conjunction with specific projects. The name of a close friend that my father had lost as the result of a drowning accident was announced. Louise said that my father was glad to have been reacquainted with him, as he would have, for this loss had been a tremendous blow. The odds that these descriptions could be dismissed as mere coincidence seemed diminished at this point.

The parallels between the events that Louise was relating at this point to those in our own lives were truly stunning. Memories that my mother and I had shared both together as well as independently with my father were expressed and directed to the one of us for whom it would hold meaning. For my mother, Louise presented images of a sloping hillside, a sort of dump or a gravel pit. She also saw my father shaking something in his hand, something like keys or a peanut, of all things, and asked if this had been a habit of his. Immediately it was obvious to my mother where the scene was, but we were both confounded by this little habit.

Mom and Dad had developed an intense interest in gold prospecting in the past few years and practiced the art of metal detecting at every opportunity. This was, in fact, their fun time. Prospecting is best practiced at old strip mining sites, which tend to resemble gravel pits with sloping sides. The place was the Forest Hill dump here in northern California where my father had in fact taken my mother for their twenty-fifth anniversary. Later we realized that Dad had kept his gold in a small glass vial in his pocket and when he had had a successful day he would pull out the vial and shake it, just like a peanut in its shell, which sounded like the jingling of keys.

For myself, Louise related a series of memories that I shared with my father as well as stories that he had shared with me throughout the years. There were images of his time in the service, of a river that Louise interpreted to be a "yucky" place with snakes. Not knowing that my father had focused his studies on reptiles and amphibians, snakes in particular, Louise had described my father's fond memory of pythons hanging in the trees above as he floated on an air mattress down a river in Vietnam. She had an image of socks being stuffed like sausages, an odd image to say the least. For my father, a field-oriented biologist, socks had for years been used as "snake bags," a way to hold and transport specimens collected in the wild.

These did not seem to be random or generic descriptions of a man whom, in desperation, I could apply to the mold of my father. These examples were very specific and directed. These are for the most part highly unique images, mind you, for the lives and interests of a wildlife biologist and his family tend to stray a bit from the norm. There was no golf, there were no suits, no ties and no office. There were only descriptions consistent with the character and nature of my father.

I was affected most by the striking way in which Louise captured my father's demeanor. The order in which she addressed specific issues was as my father would have put them. The serious yet animated fashion in which certain feelings and communications were expressed through Louise were just as my father would have expressed them. The priorities and descriptions fit a logical sequence. First were the details that would assure us of his presence and offer comfort, then the pressing issues of unfinished business that concerned my mother and me, followed by the memories and reminiscences. Finally came the new business that to me sounded just like something Dad would say.

Louise explained that in his new state, my father was seeing higher and farther beyond the physical. There was an urgency and determination expressed in sharing this state of being with those friends and colleagues with minds narrowed by the constraints of science within the physical world. If indeed my father were there, he would have been thrilled to find a means of expressing this newfound knowledge. As a man he was both a scientist and an explorer. He felt that his purpose in life was to selflessly amass and share knowledge, which as Louise explained it, seems to be the new business at hand.

Louise expressed my father's desire to point out that we limit ourselves to that with which we are familiar in this world, and in so doing compress our senses and close our minds. I've heard that we are born with an awareness of this alternate state of being, that we in fact come from there, but lose our awareness through the limits of the physical world and our existence in this life. Louise also expressed my father's desire to point out that this worldly existence is only a part of the process, and that when we leave here we have not, in fact, ceased to be.

Now, I must admit that as a student of science myself, I have had a great deal of difficulty processing and fully accepting this information. This has truly shaken the very foundations of my established beliefs. However, I may suggest that the first law of thermodynamics asserts that energy can neither be created nor destroyed. Life is fueled by energy and when the body ceases to be, there must be another destination for this energy. Yes, perhaps it is simply dispersed as heat, a less orderly phase of energy. But our senses have evolved to suit our survival in the physical world and are tuned to perceive only those things that ensure our physical existence. I would be arrogant to assume that I, as a man, am capable of comprehending all of the incredible wonders that exist within the universe.

This is how I reconcile myself with an experience that goes beyond my ability to comprehend or explain. One thing I can say with certainty is that it feels wonderful to consider that when I speak aloud to my father, there is the potential that he is there to hear me. I enjoy the thought that he did not die in vain, that his mission might continue and that a part of him remains with me as I continue on the journey that is my own life.

Eric

## AN ENLIGHTENED CYNIC

*Here is the story of another self-proclaimed skeptic. Rather than disbelieving psychic phenomena, Joe is distrustful of those who interpret this kind of information, as well as professionals who make sweeping generalizations that people tend to trust without discernment. He sought to prove me as a phony, partly because of his anger and frustration that spilled over from his attempts to meet with a more unapproachable psychic. I suspected that he had found a direction in which to vent his anger over the loss of his wife and son.*

*Joe got the proof that he sought from our session, but did not recognize it as such until a while after our meeting. Typically, arriving with specific expectations limits a client's ability to hear and identify the information that is actually being delivered. Rigid expectations can also impede the flow of information from the loved one. I can't say why loved ones at times cannot give the specific answers that the clients seek. I just know that souls on the Other Side seem to have their own agenda.*

My introduction to Louise was through a fellow griever who was in the same hospice group. We had both lost our wives in recent months. I was impressed with the enthusiastic way he described all that had transpired in his sessions with Louise.

Being an avowed cynic (one step beyond skeptic), I still felt that I must experience this sort of thing for myself. I had been trying to see another well-known individual who also was supposed to have the gift. But my failed attempts to get a response to my phone calls only increased my anger about people who claim to do this sort of thing. At the same time, I'd listened to people's stories and thought that it must be a special gift, to be able to communicate with those who move on before us.

However, I desperately wanted to make contact with my wife, Lucretia, and my son, Mark, who passed away a year and ten months before her. I'd been left with no family and with unbearable loneliness, anger and self-pity.

I had actually been contacted by my wife and son several times, in a number of different ways. I wanted confirmation from someone who was capable of tuning in.

When I arrived for the consultation with Louise, I announced that it would be quite a stretch for me to take any stock in what she might present. If you want to say that I would have to eat crow, well, I had a meal of it!

I sat through the reading, thinking that this is all great theater, some good advice and philosophy with a touch of Psychiatry 101. Then when I drove home that afternoon, I put the tape in the player, trying to listen again to all Louise had said. I actually had two tapes in hand, since I had insisted on using my own recorder along with hers, to make sure there would be no error. I turned it off, knowing that I was not ready to listen. I have to admit that at this point, I was still trying to figure out how she could have researched the information that she related to me.

Several days later, I tried to listen again and discovered both tapes had too much static to hear her clearly. She had mentioned that occasionally there is interference. Sometimes it is actually Divine Energy coming through, which can have the same effect as electrical interference.

Fortunately, I have a nephew who is a sound engineer who was able to clean up the sound and record the session onto a CD. When I finally gave up trying to challenge the information, I heard at least seventeen "revelations" that were impossible for her to know. I counted them. Here are a few of the important ones:

- She knew my son's name and when I asked how she knew, she said, "Because he's right here."
- She said that he wanted to know if I am still drawing diagrams. That is how I used to doodle when we would talk.
- She asked if he played ball because he was wearing a cap. He always wore a cap.
- He told her that his mother's favorite flower was the gardenia. She used to grow them and loved them.
- She described my bedroom with lace; the sheer curtains covering the windows on either side of the bed were lace. She also said that my bedroom was an odd shape, but I insisted that it was rectangular. Later I remembered that one corner of the room is cut off with a large Chinese screen, giving the room an appearance of a missing corner.
- She saw the full-size desk in the bedroom. She said that Lucretia knew when I was at the desk and that I went there to talk to her (which I did).
- Lucretia asked her to question me about a locket on a gold chain. It's the medallion that I wore that contained a picture of her. I had it made when we visited Holland. I called it my miraculous medal. Lucretia told her that I would know who to give it to and when to give it to the right person.

Receiving confirmation helped me trust my own ability to be in touch with my wife and son. As time passes, I don't feel them around me in the same way. Louise says that as they gain new awareness on the Other Side, they raise their vibrational frequency. That takes them to new levels and shifts their connection to this dimension, though we will always be connected. I suppose that my focus has shifted, too. I will never stop missing my son and wife, but allowing new people and experiences into my life has lessened my need to hold on to them in the old way.

One of the first experiences when I knew that I was in direct communication with my son came the night before the viewing of his body. He died from a lingering illness, and though it was a relief to have his suffering end, my wife and I missed him terribly.

Lucretia and I were lying in bed in the guest room at my sister-in-law's home. She turned to me and asked, "Where do you think Mark is now?" The moment she asked, I had the most peaceful feeling I've ever felt. My answer came so spontaneously, "He's right here."

A few moments went by, as we lay there, silently. Then we heard music playing. I was annoyed, because I couldn't find the radio or alarm clock that it might be coming from. Lucretia pointed over to a chair across the room, where she saw a light. I went over and found a musical teddy bear, which was where the music had been coming from. I told her that it was Mark, talking to us.

The next morning, my wife asked her sister about the teddy bear. She answered that it was a gift that she had set aside on the chair. She had forgotten about it. She didn't know that it could play. We looked at the label and found that it could play four songs, but it only played the one song—over and over—

"Let Me Call You Sweetheart." That was my wife's endearing name for my son. The bear has yet to play any other song.

Before we left for the viewing, we had the bear on the table, because we were going to take it with us. My niece decided to put it in a bag to keep it clean. We all left the room, then heard it play, nonstop, until she took it back out of the bag.

On the way to the viewing, I was relating a very personal story about Mark. The bear—now back in its bag, placed on the backseat—started playing again, until I stopped telling the story. I don't think that my son wanted me to tell it. Later, at the gathering after the last viewing, teddy was positioned on the table. My sister, who had been a close friend to Mark, mentally asked, "Mark, if you are here, would you please give me a sign?" The bear started to play again.

On the first Mother's Day after Mark's passing, I came downstairs and heard a tapping sound on the window in the powder room. There I found a little gray bird, pecking at the window. I went to the window and quickly reached my hand toward the bird, thinking that I would probably scare it away. Instead, it continued tapping. I called Lucretia to the window, saying, "I think that Mark wants to wish you a happy Mother's Day." She reached out to caress the spot on the window, and the bird stopped, then stared at her for a few seconds. Then it flew away. The very same thing occurred on her birthday that year.

One day, not long after my wife died, I was lying in my hammock in the backyard. I was feeling quite abandoned and alone. I said, "You know, I haven't had a sign from either of you for quite a while. How about it?"

Ten minutes later, two birds—one a cardinal, the other just like that previous gray bird—flew over my head and sat on the wire cable, about ten feet above me. They both perched there and looked at me, side by side. Lucretia's favorite bird had always been the cardinal. I knew who had sent the gray one.

Finally, a while ago, I was browsing through some photo albums in the spare bedroom. I suddenly started thinking about Mark, and how very much I missed him. Suddenly the teddy bear that I now keep in my own bedroom—two rooms away—started playing that same song. I was overcome with tears of joy that Mark was still with me—and sadness that we were no longer together in the old way.

It has been a couple of years since I saw Louise. Lucretia always felt that she would not be remembered like famous people are. Now I'm pleased to contribute my story for that reason. Now I'm an enlightened cynic.

*Joe*

## Becoming a Receiver:
## Pay Attention to the Synchronicities

Observing the synchronicities means paying attention to the "seemingly psychic timing of events" that cause you to reflect, for example, "Golly, if I hadn't gone there, I wouldn't have met so-and-so, who connected me to such and such opportunity . . ." Events that you used to call "coincidences," you begin to view as confirming evidence that a special plan is unfolding for you. You have just read about clients who connected to loved ones by paying attention to the messages they were sent through meaningful synchronicities.

Noticing the synchronicities that appear in your life will demonstrate several things. First of all, besides just being a "hoot"—a real joy to experience the unfolding of a bigger plan—noticing those moments demonstrates that you were being fully present, or you wouldn't have noticed.

Second, noticing a synchronicity is an acknowledgment that you are plugged into the Source. You are identifying that "Something else *is* going on here! There *must* be a plan!"

Third, the appearance of synchronicities will indicate that you are traveling right down the center of your path. You'll feel that your life is flowing. You'll feel less need to impose your own agenda as to how your life should evolve.

Finally, the process itself of observing synchronicities increases your multisensory ability to experience a present moment while concurrently sensing its *relevance* to a larger plan. The old way of perceiving left us experiencing random, isolated moments with little understanding of their relevance or importance to a purposeful plan. Synchronicities help you feel linked to life and are a vehicle for communication from loved ones on the Other Side, who are most definitely included in that bigger picture. Your connection is the heart-link. Your attentiveness to the synchronicities influences the extent of that communication.

One word of caution: Some clients get so excited when they start to observe synchronicities, that they interpret them as confirmation that whatsoever they desire for their lives is going to happen. Because there's the feeling that, "Whoa! Life is working!", there's the interpretation, ". . . so I can expect my life to work out my way!" Let synchronicities simply be a friendly indicator to you that a grander plan is indeed unfolding.

Think back to an event or circumstance that evolved in a remarkable way. At the time, you may have thought that the way it came about was simply a coincidence. Try to remember the details, all the quirky little turns you might have taken leading up to the event. Where were you? What was going on with you at the time? What was your frame of mind? Were there other people involved? Did it involve communication with a loved one?

See if you can recall other instances. You might not have known that these synchronicities were perfectly timed events at the time, but you might be able to see them more clearly now in retrospect. Writing them down will increase your awareness of them, make you more conscious of their appearance. They will become more identifiable to you. Pretty soon you will gain an awareness of how these synchronicities are guiding you, if they're delivering a message to you and how they relate to a much bigger plan.

# CHAPTER EIGHT

# Forgiveness

*O*ur souls journey along a continuum of consciousness that transports us in and out of the physical experience. It's an eternal existence that draws to the soul the necessary experiences from which to grow, to expand perceptions, to learn and to resolve. Life itself—and the soul experiencing it, in or out of the body—seeks resolution.

Our personal "little-self" agendas prohibit that natural progression when we feel that we have to make someone wrong—to make ourselves right—or lower another's esteem in order to elevate our own. Release to this higher level always feels wonderfully clear and oftentimes magical. It happens instantly when the heart opens to another, linking both to greater understanding and infinite possibilities.

It is never too late to resolve issues, but it's best to make use of all that "snags our sweater" here in this physical world. It is important to be attentive to the road signs that direct us to heal unresolved issues within ourselves as well as with others.

We went to a lot of effort and pain to get here! We are here to be challenged. And from the challenges, we always receive gifts. Then the Universe sends us those with whom we are to share the gifts.

The gifts that we receive often include new wisdom and learning, and increased understanding and compassion. And the ability to forgive.

I find that clients often have a hard time with the concept of forgiveness. A grown daughter received a message from her mother who had been emotionally abusive to my client until her dying day. I said, "Your mother is here to ask your forgiveness. It doesn't have to be right now. It's important that you process your anger and your feelings from the past." Brenda folded her arms in front of her, declaring, "IT'S TOO LATE!"

I replied, "It's never too late."

Then Brenda began to cry. She said that even with all the pain she still suffered from her mother's abuse, she feared that she would feel terribly guilty for seeking validation or vindication for herself. Her mother said: "It's okay to be angry with me for the things I did. It's important for you to discover how it really was for you. You're not betraying me. Your healing is my healing!"

My client, like many, felt that to forgive would be selling out, letting her mother off the hook. It would, in a sense, be an acceptance of what she'd done. Sometimes it is helpful to think in terms of release, instead of "forgiveness." When we forgive another, we release ourselves from anger and bitterness that constricts and contracts our soul's development.

I remember watching an evening news story a while ago about a group of teenagers who had just lost several good friends in a shooting by a disturbed classmate. The morning after this horrific incident, these students had draped a large banner over the school entrance that read, "WE FORGIVE YOU!"

Too soon, too fast, I thought.

A rush to forgive can be a rush to forget, to deny a deep level of pain that results from life's most challenging events. We grow tremendously when we allow the pain to lead us to a new level of our own self-discovery.

This is one way in which we become self-realized. We can start to observe a relationship between our ego-self that's playing a part here—fully engaged in the illusion of this dimension in order to be here fully as a "self"—and the soul-self that has the capacity to observe the ego-self, to surrender to the Source, and to gain wisdom and expand from an intended, greater meaning.

When we process the feelings and emotions that result from trauma, we can integrate the experience into our life. It becomes part of our soul, part of our timeless existence. Then we can gain the wisdom from the challenge and awaken to new truths as a result.

When we have done this processing, when we have identified the feelings and emotions that we're left with—such as anger, guilt, sorrow, blame, desire for revenge—then we are ready to release, to forgive another. It is a gift to ourselves when we do so.


## TYLER

*I began my presentation one particular evening at the Learning Exchange in Sacramento, California, as I usually do. I described how I receive intuitive information and what I do with it—how*

I interpret and for what purposes—and what my audience can do to become clearer receivers themselves. Then it's time to "tune in."

I usually bring through two kinds of information for random people in the group: one, a sample of a future moment where participants have gained an insight, as opposed to a future "fortune-telling" moment that will presumably jump into their laps while they sit back on their road of life; and two, messages from friends and family on the Other Side.

I first explain that I only interpret for souls who have gone to the Light—I don't do "ghost-busting"—and that when I'm sorting out their messages, I never know if they are transmitting a memory or a message. Sometimes it's very much like charades: they act out puns, handing the participant a rose (when their name was Rose). They show me old habits (like tossing popcorn in the air and catching it in their mouth) and sometimes they even show me more personal characteristics or traits.

I always trust when I do this random "tuning in" that the information I receive won't be intrusive to someone, and will always come in a way that is for their highest good. I ask for that in my invocation.

This evening at the Learning Exchange, I was tuning in to the last few people who I would approach in the audience. I walked down the aisle and felt a pull to my right, where a young woman sat on the aisle next to another woman, then a man and a boy.

At first I didn't recognize the woman who sat by her husband and son as one who I had tuned in to at a previous Learning Exchange evening six months before. Messages came in so clearly from Tyler this evening, for his whole family. It turned out to be the first experience of this kind for Kathy's husband and *son. She had coaxed them into attending that evening, with hopes that I might be able to demonstrate that their beloved Tyler was still connected to them.*

*I felt so grateful and so guided that evening. It happened perfectly and appropriately that I was "nudged" to approach this family at the end of my presentation, after Kathy's husband and son had the opportunity to get a bit desensitized, helping them to feel more comfortable with all that I would eventually give them from Tyler.*

*In the end, Tyler and his family have given us a tremendous gift: a touching example of the ability—and opportunity—to forgive. When we ask for the answers that help us process and heal the pain from our life's challenges, we are able to forgive. It's a gift to ourselves. Forgiveness releases us from bitterness, anger and fear. It balances and brings closure to old grievances. Then we are free to receive a new, more positive, expansive future.*

## First and Second Class with Louise

On March 14, 1998, my son Tyler died as a passenger in a single-car accident. He was twenty-one years old and he died just minutes from our house, the house he had lived in all his life. In my grief I was searching for a way to connect with Tyler. I just felt that he was so near and I would not have to wait until I died to hear from him and for him to hear me.

So, I attended Louise's talk by myself. This was in October of 1998. The session was just ending and I raised my hand to ask a question. When Louise came to me, she said that Tyler had just popped in beside me and was handing me a microphone. Tyler loved to sing and had a professional microphone.

She asked me if he was a comedian. I answered that he was hilarious.

The third question was the confirming one for me. She asked, "Was there something about the color yellow around him?" We have all come to think of the color yellow as a symbol of Tyler. He liked to wear these bright yellow T-shirts. We have done many things with yellow in Tyler's memory. It confirmed to me that Tyler is with us and knows what we are doing.

I anxiously waited for Louise's next talk. This was in May 1999. I brought my husband, David, Tyler's father, and my older son, Jason, Tyler's only sibling. I did feel that there was a strong chance that Tyler would contact us that night. We all have had visitation dreams from Tyler. Our bond continued to be so strong.

## The Learning Exchange

*May 24, 1999*

We arrived at the Learning Exchange classroom with hope. We were so hoping to connect with Tyler, and I (Kathy) was anxious that David and Jason would get the opportunity that I had when I attended the last talk. We had a very rewarding experience that evening.

Toward the end of the readings, Louise came to David. She said that she felt a lot of anger in David. She began by asking about David's father. Was he over-authoritative? No. Did he drink? Yes. Did he work on cars? Yes. Was David angry about his father's drinking? Not really.

David then told her about losing Tyler. Louise stated that that would certainly make you feel anger. She asked if Tyler had had a hard time breathing. (She asked this the last time I saw her.) We told her that he probably had. Louise said she had the sensation that he had been leaning to the left and slid into the accident. We said that he definitely had been leaning to the left, to try to correct the steering wheel.

Tyler was the outside passenger in a pickup truck. She then described how he hit. She said Tyler was telling her that it felt like jumping on a mattress, like the sensation as you jump and fly up. She asked if he used to jump on the beds. David answered, "Yes." He was thinking of their trips to Lee Vining, a place where the boys loved to go and where they frequently jumped on the beds. Tyler told her that was how it felt for him in the accident. It was like bouncing on the bed when he left his body.

Tyler told her a message for Jason, that "he should try it." But, then he said something on the order of "Not really!" He meant it as a joke. Tyler had a tremendous sense of humor that sometimes could be "slightly twisted" (Jason's description). Louise asked Jason if he felt guilty. Jason answered yes. She said to Jason, "Tyler is saying not to feel guilty. You do not need to. He knows that there are things that you wish you could have resolved with him."

Louise said that he had come to three out of four of us in our dreams. (Our friend Laura, who was sitting with us, was the fourth and she had not dreamed of Tyler.) Louise asked if Jason had dreamed of Tyler. Jason answered he dreamed of him all the time. Tyler said that he was with Jason often, in his sleep.

She asked if there was a child that Tyler had been close to. We said yes, thinking of Paulie, the younger brother of Stephanie. Stephanie is Tyler's former girlfriend. Then Tyler talked about us giving something of his to Paulie.

We explained that we had done just that when they came over unexpectedly the night before. It just happened to be David's birthday. David gave Paulie a trophy from when Tyler and David played on the softball team together.

Louise asked if he had some toy cars and something about boxes. Tyler's Hot Wheels cars are in boxes. Tyler was telling her they were to be for a grandchild. David and I had already decided to put the cars away and let the little visiting children play with the new cars we bought. We feel that Tyler had already communicated this to us.

She then asked about a car in the grass. Had David been working on it? We answered that the Corvette was being fixed up and that it had been in the grass. Tyler's pickup also is parked in our driveway in the grass.

She then asked about a hat. I told her about the TY hat and how we wouldn't tell anyone that the TY was for the Tampa Yankees. He would just say it is for TY! We had also given one of Tyler's best friends a TY hat just the week before.

Toward the end, Louise asked if Tyler had a collection of coins or something. Did he sneak something out and replace it? Tyler had many collections, I answered. "If he did, he may have gotten away with it." At that everyone laughed and the talk came to an end.

The experience answered some important questions for us. We were all overwhelmed with gratitude for Louise's gift that enabled us to hear from our loved and so-missed Tyler. We also are more aware that Tyler is so close and that he is able to get through to us over and over.

## Kathy's Session with Louise

*May 1999*

Louise: "Is there anything about a P.O. box? Or a locker? Or a post office?"

Kathy: "I go to the post office."

L: "Is there something you pass on the way that reminds you of Tyler every time?"

K: "The boy who was driving the car works right there, by the post office."

L: "So, he survived?"

K: "Yes."

L: "And Tyler is saying that that boy is hurting a lot."

K: "Yes."

L: "What is his name? Allen? There is the other 'A.'" (Louise had asked about two "A's.") "Have you talked to Allen?"

K: "Yes."

L: "Has it been hard to do?"

K: "Yes."

L: "Tyler is saying that it will get easier. And when you are feeling uplifted from what you are learning as a result of the loss, please bring Allen into that light. That doesn't mean you have to become evangelical.

"Now Tyler says Allen needs to know that he and Allen had been in a war together in another lifetime and the roles were reversed. He is showing me a scene on a battlefield, with him in uniform. Tyler had said, 'Go to the left!'—instead of to the right. He felt responsible for the loss of Allen's life. So his own grief caused him to bring others grief. He took his own self-scorn out on others. And he was so angry with himself that it made him angry with everybody else. It was supposed to happen this way, this lifetime. But, now Allen has to know that he can drop the ball now."

K: "Is Tyler glad about what we did in court?"

L: "What did you do? Did you release him?"

K: "We helped him."

L: "Tyler is very glad. There is something about looking through a phone book or a directory . . . or something thick. Could be like swearing on a book. Did you testify?"

K: "David spoke in court. He didn't testify."

L: "And he said?"

K: "David said that he didn't want Allen to go to jail."

L: "So you came forward in his defense?"

K: "Yes."

L: "Tyler is glad. He is so glad. He says that you had to. He was there nudging you! He's saying that Allen would have been 'done for' if he had gone to jail. He was really working hard to influence you. But your goodness did it. Your ability to forgive. And now you are passing on goodness."

K: "We told the court . . . that is what Tyler would have wanted."

L: "SEE? Because it was. He says that is exactly what he wanted. It would have carried it beyond what the lesson was for, if Allen went to jail. Not payback. Karma balances."

> (The judge had told Allen that he would be serving six months. After David read the statement, the judge said, "I'm going to do what that man asked." He did not sentence Allen to any jail time. In my reading with Louise, she said that Tyler used the words— in reference to Allen going to jail—"done for." Our family was using the word "destroyed." Another confirmation of Tyler's presence).

L: "Was Allen drinking?"

K: "Yes."

L: "Tyler says that he did something even dumber in that other lifetime. He wants you to help pull Allen out of his hole—when it feels right. He might need some background. Maybe some books about near-death experiences."

The Saturday following my private session with Louise, I attended a workshop. Following Louise's opening talk, we had exercises in remote viewing and then some short readings. Many loved ones came in for most of us. It seemed to me that Tyler came in so strongly that he was almost interrupting Louise. He wanted to tell me something. I need to explain the background in order for you to recognize the importance of what Tyler was trying to let us know.

Within a few days of the first anniversary of Tyler's death, I was driving to the post office. At the corner down the street, I thought I saw Allen, the young man who had been the driver in the accident. He was waiting to walk across the street. I got to the turning lane and realized it was Allen. I was hoping that he would not see me, as I did not feel up to talking to him at that moment. But he did see me and we waved at each other. My brother was in the car with me, and I told him that I must be supposed to talk with Allen. I stopped in the parking lot of the pizza parlor where Allen works and we hugged and talked.

I had mentioned this incident to Louise earlier, the day of the workshop. When we got to the readings, many people came through to our group. Tyler came through and talked of several things and of several of his friends.

When Louise went on to talk to others in the group, Tyler would sometimes seem to make comments. He was telling

Louise about a dry cleaners that I had passed. When she told me, I realized that it was the cleaners in the small shopping center I drove by just before I saw Allen. This was near the post office that she mentioned in my private session.

Tyler told Louise that at the time—when I was driving by the cleaners—he communicated to me to stop and talk to Allen! How wonderful!

That was one more confirmation that even though I do not consciously hear him, I am getting some messages from him. We are so connected. Many things we have learned through Louise's wonderful gift have confirmed that Tyler has communicated his wishes to us—many times.

Tyler seems very concerned about some of his friends and his brother. It helps us to know that he is so close to us. Our love is constant and forever.

Losing Tyler has been so painful. To not have him here in our daily life is to have a part of ourselves missing. We are grateful for the knowledge that he is not really gone, that he lives on and gives us comfort.

*Kathy Routt*


## "YOU PUSH, I'LL PULL"

*I've mentioned how important it is for clients to get validation for past abuse. Quite often, they've grown up learning that inappropriate behavior was acceptable—or that it didn't even exist, when the family's denial left them believing that their feelings and perceptions about the abusive behavior were inaccurate or even delusional. Inevitably, they have a very difficult time trusting what they feel, even knowing what they feel, in the present.*

*I once looked into a client's childhood and saw horrific abuse. Her father was out of control, yelling and screaming while beating up my client and her two brothers. In one instance, I watched him wreaking havoc in the kitchen, throwing pots and pans all over the place. I described all of this to my client. She responded, emotionless, "Oh, that was Daddy just having a good time." Then I saw a scene of her at bedtime. Her mother was sitting on the side of her bed, saying, "That was your Daddy just having a good time." I went on to discover that this woman was clearly out of touch with the important issues that were disrupting her life in the present.*

*I had seen something similar years before, reading another client who exhibited absolutely no emotions, showed no expression on her face; she seemed completely shut down. When I spoke to her upon her arrival for her consultation, she seemed very distracted, only partly there. Later in the session, when I looked into her childhood, I watched her father carrying a butcher knife. It's difficult for me to interpret that which has not been included in my repertoire of experiences. I am grateful that violence has not been part of my life. I thought the man might have worked in a butcher shop.*

*"Daddy used to come at us with a butcher knife," my client said flatly.*

*Then I described a scene of someone being locked in a closet. Again, emotionless, dissociated from her feelings, my client responded, "Oh, my brothers used to lock me in a closet where someone had been murdered." I talked to her for a while about my thoughts regarding her needing some therapeutic counseling. I felt that she had some very critical issues to deal with, so much to heal that had been buried for so long.*

*Later I mentioned a potential future moment, should she be able to tend to these issues. I described the setting, and added, "And here, you're feeling happy about a new project that you're implementing in a different job, where your employer is kind and fair.* We had already established that she was playing out some unresolved drama about her father with her current, abusive employer. She said, "You say feelings, and I just feel confused." Just the thought of feelings was baffling to my client.

*This is why validation is so important. However, a balance must be achieved in processing the anger and emotions that fester (the negativity from the past) and then allowing in the positive, when it's appropriate and healthy to do so. The following is an example of how my client was able to heal even beyond the effects of necessary validation, by trusting an intuitive sense that something more was being offered. She sensed that she would benefit from receiving something back from her father. It became clear to her that holding on to her anger might be blocking her own potential to expand.*

The time that my father and I spent together in this lifetime was tumultuous. He was alcoholic, and his disease progressed with every year that I grew into adulthood. Most of my memories of my father were of his rage, cruelty and razor-sharp wit. After he passed, he came to me often in my dreams. He usually appeared to be sober, but my reaction to him was very negative, as if he had not changed. Many nights, I woke in tears after screaming at him, "I'm glad you're dead! Life is better for all of us without you. I hate you!"

When I connected to him in my session with Louise, which took place one year after his passing, she showed me that he was coming to me in those dreams so that I could vent my anger, to say those very things and get past our difficult times. He was doing this to validate me, Louise said.

My father was able to say how much he regretted his shortcomings, and reminded me that we did share some good times. My anger had made it impossible to remember anything positive about my dad. No pleasant memories remained. But he reminded me of a time before his alcoholism controlled him, when I was around the age of seven. I used to eagerly await his arrival home from work, when we would go swimming together in our backyard pool. I loved to sit on his shoulders and he'd dive under the water, like a submarine. That's the scene that he showed Louise. Dad was giving me back what I now hold as one of my fondest memories.

In my last session with Louise, she said that my father was showing her a picture of a woman sitting in a car, parked by a swimming pool. The woman looked very sad, her head resting on the steering wheel. I told her it was me she was seeing, last week. I was parked by the pool at the school where I work. I did not want to go in to work that day. I was tired of working, unhappy at my job. Then I remembered that I had suddenly thought of my dad at that time. Louise said that he wanted me to know that he'd been there with me, extending his love and support.

It seems that now on the Other Side, my father is able to be the loving father that he was unable to be in his life on earth. I'm finally able to accept his love. This has healed me of my wounds, and I believe it has helped him to evolve on the Other Side.

After making that connection—now that I'm able to understand what my father wanted me to know—I have been open and available to our bond of love. I now feel him with me daily, talk with him constantly and can even, once again, enjoy his humor. It is not infrequent that I find myself "thinking like him," and it brings a huge smile to my face.

An example of his humor came in my last session with Louise. She said that my father would be helping my elderly grandmother to the Light when her time comes. He said that my grandmother was terrified of dying. He wanted me to assure her that there's nothing to fear, to help her prepare for her transition. Louise said that he was saying, "You push, I'll pull."

## Becoming a Receiver: Surrender to the Source

There came a day several years ago when "the Voice" said to me, "Now it's time to show people where they've known God." I was meditating between consultations that I was doing for a week in a small town in Colorado. The message was unmistakable. I didn't attempt to figure out how that instruction would manifest in my life, but simply stayed open to however the message might reveal itself.

Gradually I started noticing a new element working its way into the consultations. After reciting my invocation, then scanning the information to interpret, I would occasionally view a spark or flash of light come into the client's past, present or probable future. As I looked further into where I'd seen the flash, a scene would appear. Sure enough, when I'd describe what I was watching to clients, they would usually recall that past or present moment when they felt extremely connected to life, part of the whole picture, or unusually serene or peaceful. But most often, they hadn't defined the moment as "knowing God."

When the flash appeared in a future moment for one client, I advised her to stay open to it coming in on its own, in its own way. She is a stockbroker on Wall Street, and that particular future moment found her in the middle of a meeting with colleagues. I gave her the initials—and in a couple of cases, the names—of those who would be in the room with her at the time. I felt—through her future consciousness—the sensation of extreme clarity, an opportunity where she would feel compelled to speak her truth in a way that would make a difference.

This is a wonderful thing to be able to demonstrate to clients, because so many tend to hope and pray for unmistakable evidence that they are connected, that God is near. Sometimes they even secretly hope for a near-death experience, asking to take on potentially unimaginable pain and anguish! It's hard for them to trust that they are already connected, in their very own, personal, unique way, but they have never defined a particular feeling or event as evidence. The tendency is, so often, to go outside ourselves for answers and confirmation, when we don't realize that we've been connected all along in our own God-given way.

Occasionally I invite the flash, asking telepathically during the consultation to see where this client has known God.

For one client, the moment I viewed was when he was in fourth grade, fishing on the lake with his Uncle Joe. He remembered the moment, feeling loved and at one with everyone and everything around him.

Trust the moments where you felt connected to the Source in your very own, unique and personal way. Surrender to your own perception of a Higher Power or higher consciousness. Watch for a tendency to "play God in your head." None of us are equipped to figure out solutions—or a better plan for our life—alone, through our rational, deductively reasoning mind. Your mind is a treasure and an incredible gift. It allows you to experience and interpret your physical world. But it cannot interpret intuitive information in a rational way. Your ego-self will resist releasing control of script-writing your life. It can only provide a script that will greatly narrow the possibilities in a truly infinite plan.

A few years ago, my daughter called one evening from where she lives in another country, requesting something of me that I wasn't able to deliver at the time. "But sweetheart," I said, "I will pray for you." "Thanks, Mom," she replied, as she hung up. I went to my knees to pray for her and for a friend who was about to have surgery for colon cancer. I prayed and prayed and prayed. Then I heard "the Voice" say to me, "NOW IT'S TIME TO STOP!"

It was so clear to me at that moment that I was, in a sense, playing God. If I could get it just right, ask long and eloquently enough, I might receive all that I was asking for, in just the way that I desired. I realized that to continue praying in this way was a demonstration of my disbelief that my prayer would be heard! I needed to release to the Source, to infinite possibilities that I cannot begin to fathom. Releasing is a demonstration of faith.

It was simply enough for me to put forth my intention—from the heart—and then release my thoughts, my worries and any expectations of how I thought events should transpire. I forced myself to crawl into bed and let my last thoughts before sleep be only thoughts of gratitude. My daughter called the next day to report some wonderful—and unexpected—synchronicities that had transpired that morning.

We are addicted to attempting to control our lives because we fear the unexpected. The best and quickest antidote to fearful thoughts that constrict is to think thoughts of gratitude, which expand. Surrendering to the Source made me feel connected once again. It also took matters out of my mind-self's limited capacity to solve problems and let the Universe work its magic. The heart-link to the Source is found in the same place within you that connects you to loved ones on the Other Side.

Feel (or ask to feel) infinite, unconditional love from the Source. Let it surround you. Whenever I make this request, then I surrender completely and wait patiently, quietly. It always comes. It's the most wonderful feeling. You'll never feel alone, once you have felt it.

---

## TRY THIS

Make a list of moments when you felt connected to the Source, to a Higher Power. You might not have defined those instances in terms of having been connected. A particular moment might have found you in nature, momentarily losing awareness of your physical self, feeling expanded and fully alive. There might have been a moment when you spontaneously reached out to another, maybe even a stranger—almost in spite of yourself— and felt yourself extremely connected to that person. Taking inventory of these moments will increase your ability to identify them as they are occurring in the present—mid-experience— as well as in retrospect. This will increase the times you actually have this kind of experience!

---

CHAPTER NINE

# Getting "Dialed"

*I*n most of the stories you've read, my clients were assisted in trusting their own increasing intuitive abilities and their special heart-link connection to loved ones by receiving confirmation in consultations about specific moments when they suspected that they were indeed connected. That is the first step to becoming a receiver, being able to trust that you are receiving. One apprentice cleverly refers to her feelings of being "tuned in," or receiving accurately, as being "dialed."

The most intuitive "hits" are the ones that come out of left field, out of the blue. See if you can follow a thread from what you suspect to be an intuitive hit, back to previous thoughts that you were entertaining. If it's an isolated symbol, vision or thought, it could be a reliable sensing. Try to recollect how you felt when it came in. You were most likely "in neutral," feeling relaxed and detached from trying to get a hit.

For example, you might have been walking down the street, when you passed a shop where you and your mother used to shop. You looked in the window, and there you saw a red coat on the mannequin, just like the one you gave her for her last birthday before she passed over. You thought of her, then suddenly, you felt her. You may have suddenly received a vision of her face, of her smiling at you. Most likely, she was doing so! The environmental stimuli triggered thoughts of your mother that took you to the heart-link that connected you. You might even recall synchronicities that led you down that street in the first place, as in the experience of Tyler's mom in chapter 8.

When you try too hard to receive, you pollute the images or sensings. It takes practice and increasing self-trust to hold on to a perception longer and sense its validity. Our instinctive reaction to intuitive information is frequently, "Oh, I just made that up. It's just my imagination." Observe these thoughts of doubt, and then release them.

Hold on to that intuitive hit. Communicate it, write it down, check it out with others as soon as you can. The sooner you bring it forth—"give it off"—the less chance your rational mind will have to doubt and dismiss.

The second step involves interpreting the information accurately. In chapter 1, I mentioned the example of the client who misinterpreted the feeling of a deep, past-life connection to a married man whom she met. She interpreted that feeling as evidence that they were supposed to be together. She could trust that sensing of a deep connection, but instead she might have looked to how their paths had configured this lifetime— making them unavailable to each other in an intimate way—to help her interpret that they were to support each other in a new way. Then she would surrender (all of her expectations) to the Source, "asking to be shown" and remembering to watch for synchronicities and cues from the Universe that would guide her.

Another way that I help further clients' growth into multisensory, intuitive beings is through an ongoing apprenticeship program that I conduct over a six-month period with a few select clients at a time. I conduct the program over the phone with clients from around the world.

Apprentices fax me their dreams and together we work to interpret communication from their unconscious. We explore remote viewing, sensing beyond linear time and opening up communication from the physical to the nonphysical dimension. Occasionally I interpret for an apprentice's child-self—still existing in the past—who might raise his/her hand to be called on, so to speak. Sometimes this occurs in order for an apprentice to address an old fear, belief or past issue that rears its head as the result of shifting and expanding perceptions in the present.

My intention is to eventually have a group of very intuitive, graduated apprentices who will be well equipped to pass along the tools that we've developed by working together, tools that are helping them become truly multisensory. That time is near.

Many people do receive confirmation from scheduling consultations. You will want to interview prospective psychics, intuitives, spiritual counselors to get a feel for their particular philosophy and spiritual perspective. It is becoming increasingly less phenomenal that there are those who can "read" and interpret this kind of information—from beyond time and death. Since so much importance is in the actual interpretation, it is crucial to find a reader/counselor who has a positive outlook rather than one who projects a mysterious and dark demeanor. Additional important factors include their ability to interpret in ways that are accurate and specific (rather than nonspecific generalizations), empowering (rather than flattering) and relevant to your life in the present.

*The next two stories are good examples of clients who trusted the information that they were receiving through visions, symbols and dreams.*

## CAROLYN'S DREAM

When I was a child, the prospect of going to sleep was so exciting for me. I dreamed such colorful and entertaining dreams. Throughout my life, the dreams have changed, but they have never faded or become less interesting. If I had a particularly interesting or funny dream, I would share it with my mother.

After I moved away, I would call her once a week; our conversations usually included my sharing of special dreams. My mother knew that I was attentive to my dreams and kept a dream journal. So it wasn't surprising when, after her death, I began dreaming dreams that included her.

My mother's death left me bereft and so saddened that I would break down and cry at the slightest thought of her. I sought out Louise to help me understand this stage of grief and to effect some communication with my mother. I had known Louise Hauck since 1992, and she had become a dear friend, not only an intuitive with whom I had consultations. I knew that if there were anyone who could help me to get a grip on this grief, it would be her.

Louise brought my mother forward in consultations and helped me to communicate with her. Many of these sessions helped to ease the pain, but I still needed something more. In one session, Louise mentioned that if I stayed open and receptive, my mother would come to me in a dream. That must have been the suggestion that I needed.

I started to dream about my mother and receive messages from her. She must have remembered that I paid a lot of attention to my dreams, finding it the most direct way to communicate with me. Sometimes the dreams had very distinct messages; sometimes she simply stood in the wings of the dream stage, as with the following dream.

In February of 1999, I had scheduled an outing with a friend who lived about sixty miles from my home. I was really looking forward to the meeting. The morning that I was to leave, just before awakening, I received a very striking image— as clear as a picture or a postcard. I knew that my mother had sent it.

I remembered that the dream didn't really include her, but she was standing off to the side as if waiting for the right moment to send me a message. The picture flashed up on the screen of my dream stage, filling it completely with no distractions.

The image was of a black and red love seat, very straight backed like a bench. As I awoke, I thought how strange this was, since I didn't think the love seat was particularly attractive, nor one that I would choose. I wrote about it in the dream journal that I keep by my bed. Then I filed the image away in my mind for future reference.

I was late, as usual, and hurried to my friend's house. I picked her up, took her to lunch and then we decided to go antiquing. As we entered an antique shop, directly in front of me was the black and red couch that I had seen in my dream! I hadn't told my friend about the dream, so I simply approached the couch and rested my hand on it. It was actually an old carousel seat from a merry-go-round, which was now being merchandised as a couch. I was perplexed since this looked like the couch in my dream. But why was I seeing it here? What was the message? I continued to browse, finding a few items to purchase. I stepped into line at the counter to pay for them.

The woman who managed the store asked the man ahead of me if he was looking for anything specific. I heard him laugh, saying that he wouldn't know where to begin, his list was so long. It made me think about an antique artist's stool I'd wanted for a long time. I had even given my mother a sketch of it, in case she might find one in her travels. We both used to love to putter through antique stores together.

After the initial thought about the stool, I decided to go ahead and ask the manager about it. It seemed impractical to do so, living so far away and not having seen anything that resembled it in the store. I was writing out a check for my items, when I suddenly blurted out, "There is something I'm looking for." This is so uncharacteristic of me, usually feeling quite shy about asking for things. I was surprised at my outburst, but nevertheless, continued on to tell the woman about the stool. She said, "Wait a minute."

She pulled a piece of paper from the counter drawer and drew the exact stool I'd been searching for! She said that her partner, a woodworker, had sold it to an artist. The artist had called her just the day before, asking if he could bring it back for a refund. He was falling on hard times and needed the money.

I asked if I could see the stool. The woman called her partner at her studio, learning that the gentleman had just returned it, whereupon she discovered that one of the legs was broken. She would have to repair it before reselling it.

Feeling excited, I turned to my friend to ask if she had the time for us to go see the stool. She was happy to accommodate me. The store manager drew us a map and off we went to the woodworker's studio.

There, standing in the studio, was the exact stool I had been looking for, long before my mother had died. It needed to be repaired and relieved of a terrible paint job. The wood-worker promised me a beautiful stool.

As we left the studio, I began to recount to my friend the story of the black and red couch and how my mother had sent me the image in a dream. My friend believes as I do, that our loved ones on the Other Side are never lost, that we are forever connected through our hearts. This story didn't seem so strange to her. She had lost a son who had connected with her in her dreams.

I told her that I thought the image of the red couch directed me to the antique artist's stool, like a clue on a treasure map. Mom would have done something like that. That was her style. She did things like that for birthdays when my siblings and I were young.

I didn't hear from the woodworker for months, and I decided that perhaps I had exaggerated the importance of all the signs from my mother. Then I received a call from the woman. She apologized for the delay, caused by a trip to Europe. She would have the stool completed sometime in June, she said. A little later she did call, announcing that it was fin-ished and looking beautiful.

I panicked; temporarily low on pin money, I couldn't spare the extra for the stool at that time. We agreed upon a pickup date the following month—it turned out my husband was happy for the opportunity to buy me the perfect birthday gift. He appreciated the whole dream story.

Two years before my mother's death, she and I had perused an antique store in northern Michigan, where we found an old drawing board. She had said then that she wanted to buy it for me for my birthday. She promised later to find an artist's stool to go with it. And though she may not have been able to personally hand it to me in a physical way, I believe that she finally led me to the stool with the simple image of a black and red couch, sent to me in a dream.

*Carolyn*

## THE MONEY TREE

*The two most recent times Linda had consultations, her father appeared, trying to communicate something about trees. The first time he did this, I asked, "Did he have something to do with trees?"*

*"Well, yes, I guess so. Dad came from a family of loggers in the Northwest," Linda responded. "Logging and trees were how they made their living." Then she added, "But he often said, 'Money does not grow on trees.' He meant it. But it was also a joke, since our last name is Money!" She thought for a moment, then said, "Oh dear. Do you think that he's trying to tell me that I'm not spending wisely?"*

*In Linda's next session, once again, her father appeared, and once again, pantomiming something about a tree! I went on to interpret other things, but her dad kept distracting me about this trees thing. I focused my full attention on him, telepathically asking, "What is it about trees?"*

Then the scene shifted. Now Linda's father was shaking a tree. Then the tree leaves became coins. Then the coins became silver dollars. They reminded me of the leaves on the aspen trees in Colorado. I described all of this to Linda.

"Oh!" she exclaimed. "I'll bet he's 'talking' about his silver dollar collection! It's tucked away in the basement. He collected the coins forever, since the war. It was his hobby. He felt that each coin meant something. In some cases, the coins would be a mint set for the year of a family member's birth. There are hundreds of them in cigar boxes and old coffee cans. He stuffed them into anything that would hold their weight. My sister and I couldn't bear to sell them, since they were so precious to him."

When I asked Linda's father if he wanted them to sell the coins, he gave me a thumbs-up gesture and smiled. Then he said, "I don't need them! They can help to bring some financial ease to my family."

Linda laughed, "Dad always was so concerned about money matters!"

Linda is easy to read, because she understands how messages often come to me in symbols or images that have to be interpreted. She herself is able to interpret this kind of communication. Because her rational mind doesn't force her to disregard sensings that aren't concrete or obvious, she is a natural receiver for this sort of nonlinear, abstract information.

Besides demonstrating Linda's trust in her ability to receive and decipher messages from loved ones, her story also shows how she had to meet her parents on their terms. Rather than demanding proof of their visits in ways that she might specify, she was open and receptive to however they were able to reach *her. In a sense, she met them halfway, without preconceived notions of how the messages would come about.*

∞

A few years ago, I was scheduled to leave for Stuttgart, Germany, to perform annual training as a reservist in the U.S. Army. I didn't want to leave my mother, who was having a difficult time adjusting to life without my father. He had died the year before, after forty-seven years of marriage.

Mom and I had agreed that there was no good time for me to leave and that I must go. We made arrangements for her to stay with her brother while I was gone, so I was able to leave with a little less apprehension.

I had been in Germany for one and one-half weeks, distracted by a feeling of not wanting to be there. Then I was notified that my mother had suffered a heart attack. When I asked if I should come home, I was told that it was unnecessary to do so. But the following week my family called to say that things were not going as they should. The doctors were quite concerned about Mom's condition.

I remember thinking that things probably were going the right way for Mom. When Dad died, she mentioned that should she ever become critically ill, she wanted no extraordinary measures performed. I understood, and felt the same. I told her that even if I could not be standing by her when her time came, I knew that she would come to me, somehow, and let me know. She laughed, then muttered, "You're probably right."

I knew this, because that's exactly what my father had done, moments before his death. I felt him, as if he was grasping my shoulder, instructing me to pick an appropriate dress for his funeral. I knew it was Dad, because he used to get my attention in the same way. Still, on the flight home, I prayed hard, thinking that if I prayed enough, I might get to see Mom one more time.

My eyes were closed while in prayer, my head leaning against the airplane window. I was crying but felt very peaceful. While in prayer I saw a vision of two geometric shapes walking toward me. I knew that one was female, the other male. There was no doubt that the woman was my mom. She was coming to let me know that her time had come.

In a brief moment, it felt as though I were three years old. Mom was bending over me to kiss me on the forehead—the way she used to do—to say good-bye. She said that she loved me. The man took Mom's hand and walked away into a lemon-yellow-white light. The man was my dad. It was so clear to me that the geometric shapes were the essence of his thoughts. He wanted to tell me that it was he who came for Mom, and that everything was all right.

Suddenly I felt incredible love when they walked into the Light. That's when I understood Dad's message, that everything was fine. I did not want to know what Dad was showing me, but I could accept that Dad was helping Mom over. They would now be together. I called the hospital from the plane phone to make sure that Mom had last rites, since our family is Catholic.

I spoke to a nurse who told me my mother was a very sick woman. I didn't know how to tell her I already knew. I asked her to tell Mom that I was on my way home and that I loved her. My mother died shortly after I landed. I never saw her alive again.

My parents' death has taught me that dying is the most painful for the living. Death creates gaps for those of us who are left on this earth, ones that we want to fill. We want to explain things beyond this world with provable facts. I feel that if I had been focused on facts, I would have missed the comfort that both of my parents brought me in such a loving way. My dad could not have been more obvious in choosing geometric shapes to communicate. I know that's how he used to think. We used to talk about it.

Since that time, I have heard Dr. Raymond Moody speak about empathic death experiences. His evidence confirmed that people are reporting more and more experiences like mine, especially when there is a close bond—a heart connection—between two people.

*Linda*

## Becoming a Receiver:
## Trust Your Ability to Connect with Loved Ones

In numerous consultations, loved ones on the Other Side show me specific times and places where they have "linked" with clients. They do this in order to help clients trust what they felt in those moments, sensations they may have doubted. An important aspect of my work lies in simply confirming for individuals that the messages, the feelings of connecting they've experienced, are true.

The heart connects to loved ones in quiet moments, while looking at a picture in a frame on a nightstand or on a wall. It happens when smelling the scent of a loved one's favorite flower or perfume. It happens when viewing a scene that brings that soul to mind. It happens when something funny occurs that reminds you of that person's humor. Humor most certainly opens the heart.

Feeling gratitude links you immediately to a loved one. Departed souls often say to clients in consultations, "If you want us to come to you in a dream, let your last thoughts before sleep be thoughts of gratitude. This creates the frequency that opens your heart and lets us come through more clearly." Thoughts of fear or yearning constrict and shut them out because those thoughts close off the heart connection.

When you dream that you have been with a soul that is no longer in the physical dimension—a very lucid, clear dream—you have indeed been "hanging out" together. You go in and out of your body frequently in your sleep. When you feel a jolt or jar yourself in your sleep, your etheric or "light body" is simply coming back into your body too quickly, or you have come back in lopsided.

Loved ones come to us in quiet places such as cemeteries, religious places or special places that you've shared, because in that moment your thoughts are directed toward them. These are places where you connect because those locations remind you of the feeling of being connected. You feel connected from your heart, and then suddenly, you are.

When you start to trust these feelings, you will begin to see more and more ways that your loved ones communicate with you through images, thoughts and personal signs. Let this happen gently, without expectations. Trying too hard at this will have you second-guessing yourself. These messages and visitations are delightful and uplifting; they float into your consciousness gently—as if on a light, puffy cloud—and then they move on.

Go to your special place. Quiet yourself. Surround yourself with the Light. Begin with an invocation or a prayer. Then open your heart to a loved one who has left the physical dimension. Feel loving thoughts about that soul or recall precious memories. Try to visualize this soul. Or just pretend that you're seeing him/her. When you feel a shift, an opening, a deep sensation, you are suddenly linked. Your loved one isn't coming in from some "place." Opening your heart creates the frequency that links you instantly, through timeless, never-ending consciousness. This feeling will become more and more discernable and unmistakable.

# Epilogue

$\mathscr{I}$ was nearing completion of this book when my good friend Harry died in his sleep from a heart attack. At the time, I was on the road, doing talks and consultations in Virginia, through Richmond, Manassas and Alexandria. Receiving the news was a shock, and it was a challenge to "keep on truckin'," doing all that I was committed to do on my trip while grieving the loss of my dear friend.

I had lost relatives, and that is a deep hurt. But never a friend, a child or a partner. With a beloved friend I have shared a rhythm of life, I have shared in play and in mutual support during times of challenge. A friend stimulates and complements me with differing perspectives and enlivens me with whatever he or she feels passionately about. A male friend anchors me when my intuitive, creative, visionary self takes over and needs to be grounded. A female friend knows how that feels.

My life has been deepened now, grieving the loss of a special friend. It has increased my compassion for the clients who sit before me, some of whom are struggling to keep marching while they grieve for a loved one. I'm learning how to acknowledge and allow myself to feel the void, the pain that will inevitably increase my capacity to feel more joy. We are here to feel fully in this physical dimension.

It is unusual for me to experience grief while being the recipient—rather than the deliverer—of wonderful, synchronistic signs that are sent to us to confirm that we are watched over and that the heart-link with another is never lost. One of my apprentices said it beautifully, "The shift and realization of that which is lost and that which is gained leaves us feeling sad one moment and a bit giddy the next."

I met Harry my first New Year's Eve after moving to Manhattan. I felt a nudge to get out and about, and took the subway to check out the film library at Lincoln Center. Then I made my way across Broadway in search of a good bowl of soup. That's where I met Harry—at O'Neal's—this handsome man with gorgeous white hair and a dazzling smile. But it was his hearty laugh that prompted me to turn in his direction on my right and ask him subway logistics for my return trip. Later, we stepped out into the street to watch the midnight fireworks together. It was the beginning of a wonderful, very special friendship.

Harry knew how to "work the room," delivering bear hugs to backstage buddies, writers, dancers, musicians, locals from the neighborhood, and employees from ABC and NBC. Harry was cool. Some of his friends called him, "The Man." Everyone loved his showbiz stories, recounting the days of illuminating the stage for Jimmy Durante (his favorite), Frank Sinatra and Tony Bennett. He infused smoke onto a stage where Charlton Heston was making his first live TV appearance, as a character sitting in the facsimile of a fizzling electric chair. Harry received a cigarillo from Basil Rathbone and toured with Angela Lansbury. He took dinner breaks down the street—oftentimes sitting next to Larry Hagman—where Bruce Willis tended bar.

One evening Harry and I practiced telepathy at O'Neal's. I "sent" him the song "Ebony and Ivory." He smiled, then started playing the table, like a piano. He was extremely intuitive. Fascinated by metaphysical principles—welcoming the concept that our lives do relate to a greater plan—he enthusiastically passed around my Intro Tape to his friends. When he first heard it, he said, "I really like that word you came up with, 'enlightenment.'" As if I thought of it!

Harry was intrigued by the exercise I suggest on the tape: to "visualize putting all your cares and worries in the basket of a big, beautiful air balloon, seeing it lift up into the sky, releasing from your consciousness to a higher level of resolution." At first, Harry confessed that when he tried the exercise at night, just before sleep, it was a bit unnerving to cut the string and let his worries float away. He preferred to tether it. Eventually he would report amazing "serendipitous" events that would result when he let go. Whenever it was time to part, after having dinner together during Harry's break between shows, I would say to him, "Harry! Go forth and illuminate!"

Harry occasionally shared details about his more rough-and-tumble days, during the years before I met him. He seemed relieved when I told him that I didn't think that he'd be going to a less than holy place when it was his time. He was happy to hear that he'd one day meet up with some of his buddies who had gone on before him—sooner than we ever imagined.

Our lifestyles and our pasts differed dramatically; we came from—and lived in—two very different worlds. Yet our paths crossed, our hearts connected, and in doing so, we created the link that now connects us eternally, beyond time and space.

Harry and I have been in communication since his passing. He visits in my dreams and he sends telepathic messages for me to deliver to his family and his friends. His family is also experiencing confirmation of their lasting connection to Harry, through some entertaining synchronicities. It's as if he is still working his magic backstage.

This is what is available to all of us when we open up to a new perception about the nature of our timeless existence, when we observe "self" from the perspective of the soul, when we take responsibility for the choices we make—choosing wiser ones after learning from less effective ones—when we trust the intuitive gifts that are part of our natural, multisensory nature, and finally, when we surrender to the Source.